MW01289929

REACH Presentation Skills

By

Peter W. Carbone
561.704.3647
www.MagnanimousConsulting.com

T.A.R.A.
(To Always Reach Above)

authorHOUSE®

AuthorHouse™
1663 Liberty Drive, Suite 200
Bloomington, IN 47403
www.authorhouse.com
Phone: 1-800-839-8640

All rights reserved. No part of this book may be reproduced or transmitted in any form or by any means, electronic or mechanical, including photocopying, recording or by any information storage and retrieval system, without written permission from the author, except for the inclusion of brief quotations in a review.

© 2007 Peter W. Carbone, MBA. All rights reserved.

No part of this book may be reproduced, stored in a retrieval system, or transmitted by any means without the written permission of the author.

First published by AuthorHouse   12/11/2007

ISBN: 978-1-4343-3039-0 (sc)

Library of Congress Control Number: 2007905635

Printed in the United States of America
Bloomington, Indiana

This book is printed on acid-free paper.

Peter W. Carbone is the sole author of the short stories, poetry and context of this book: REACH Presentation Skills.

Bible quotes come from the NIV Counselor's NEW TESTAMENT and PSALMS ZONDERVAN BIBLE PUBLISHERS

Hershey's story is from my research conducted at Hershey Park, Hershey, PA and the historical materials they had throughout the park for public knowledge.

I like to express much appreciation to Monsignor Frank Hendrick, who has truly lived magnanimously.

Table of Contents

REACH

I REACH and REACH up toward the sky

where there are no limits. (I wonder why?)

I mean, I know my limitations, I'm only a man;

Yet, I REACH for something because I know that I can!

Like drops of water dripping on rocks.
Like one man netting the worth of Fort Knox.
Nature, with water, breaks rocks to mere sand;
And that one man "made it" because he said, "I can!"

There are no limits, if there were, I'd be through.

There would be nothing to embrace and nothing to do.

No one can tell me that I have no vision,

My destiny is out there and I must continue my mission.

So I go out to the ocean, to the edge of the beach,

I extend my right hand and I continue to REACH!

Peter W. Carbone

I will enter this day and add beauty to the world. I will welcome others with a quiet love that cannot be heard, but only felt the moment their eyes engage mine. It is then that I will breakdown their armor that shields them from me. For, I will see them, and they, me.

Just as we can open our eyes, look up and marvel at the infinite and glorious universe above, we must learn to close our eyes and see the infinite universe and all its treasures that are hidden inside each of us. There is a unique universe within our respective bodies that plays host to our talents, experiences, emotions and boundless imaginations. This beautiful universe is our gift from God. We store and nurture our universe, within, in the same way I envision God stores and nurtures our universe above. We become witness to God's universe whenever we gaze from earth to heaven.

Become witness to your universe. Go exploring and travel into the vastness of yourself. Discover uncharted depths and relearn forgotten paths. Unlock that chest of drawers and marvel at your forgotten childhood treasures. Touch areas you have yet to touch. Feel your heart beat to a rhythm as it creates a song that is given to you for your life. Listen to your breath as it joins your song in harmony; it is this song that celebrates your life. Caress your soul as if it is the first time you two have ever met. Entangle yourself with your soul and dance with it! Dance and pulsate to every beat your song has to offer. Dance freely and passionately and don't be afraid of, but be surprised by, your radiance. Don't be bound to any form or technique and don't be inhibited. Just dance, fervently, freely and intimately with steps that are light, graceful and free. Journey your life, encounter all your gifts and then share them with the simple but important purpose of adding beauty to the world.

Communicate the following: I will enter this day and add beauty to the world. I will welcome others with a quiet love that cannot be heard, but only felt the moment their eyes engage mine. It is then that I will breakdown their armor that shields them from me. For, I will see them and they, me.

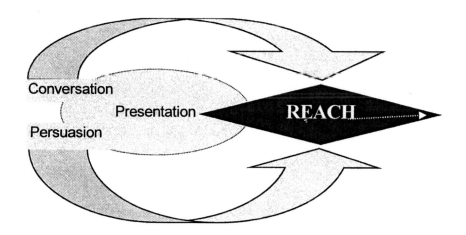

Prelude

> *He appeared in a body, was vindicated by the Spirit, was seen by angels, was preached among the nations, was believed on in the world, was taken up in glory.*
>
> TIMOTHY 3:16

Do you have the confidence to articulate your beliefs and thoughts to others?

Imagine what life must have been like for Paul, the Apostle to the Gentiles, two thousand years ago. After being rebuked by many a naysayer while he was being true to the teachings of Jesus Christ, Paul embarked on three missionary journeys to preach Christianity. Paul was teaching a religion that few, at that time, had experienced. In fact, he not only preached Christianity, he also recruited Christians who were later responsible for handing down the teachings of Jesus for generations to follow. He made it his mission to preach to strangers and non-believers while enduring many a tribulation for the sake of a Christian life and Christian doctrine.

Envision the daunting, nonetheless, incredible responsibility this effort must have been for Paul and his followers. He must have come up against many a naysayer, yet was quite successful persuading people and moving their spirits, hearts, and minds toward Christ. Imagine the impressive presentation skills Paul presumably had to be able to successfully pass along Christianity at this pivotal religious period. Paul's communication abilities proved triumphant, as he is known for "strengthening the disciples and encouraging them to remain true to the faith. 'We must go through many hardships to enter the kingdom of God'" (Acts 14:22). In fact, Paul was so successful that he, with the help of others, is known to have "opened the door of faith to the Gentiles" (Acts 14:27). He convinced many to endure their adversities, continue with their mission, and maintain their faith.

Were Paul and the others victorious with articulating their beliefs and thoughts? Absolutely, today there are over two billion Christians in the world, which demonstrate Paul's success. There are over two billion Christians, which illustrates that Paul, the Apostle to the Gentiles, knew how to be great and inspire!

Fact, an effective presenter will rely on the combination of impressive conversation skills and persuasive skills to transport herself from one location of a presentation to another, much like a cyclist will rely on a combination of tires to transport herself from one location to another. This notion is true, however, many people don't rely on the nuances of these two important skills during his or her presentation. Combinations such as the aforementioned simply make sense. The improvements on your skills of conversation and persuasion will enhance your ability to present effectively. Therefore, it is important to ramp up each of these skills so the combination of the first two will help you with your third, the skill to present. In essence, many people need to learn how to REACH Presentation Skills and utilize those skills so they can, in turn, be great and inspire; thus the nature of this book.

Section one refers to the importance of choosing the right word(s) while we are in conversation with others. This is the Power of Conversation. Not only is it imperative to choose the right word(s), it is equally important to choose the right delivery. The first section stresses the importance of enhancing the skill of conversation because without this skill, one will not be able to effectively REACH Presentation Skills to the level that one will inspire others, which is the principal reason for presenting. The skill to converse is a learned skill, which must be treated with high regard because we humans are dependent on this skill.

For example, parenting is developing the future, via, our children. Moreover, parenting is coaching and salesmanship. The better equipped one is to accomplish any task, the more efficient one is and the greater probability one will realize success. Communication is a means to action and accomplishment. People will respond to the way in which you choose your words; therefore, choose judiciously. People will respond to the way in which you choose your delivery; therefore, choose judiciously.

Section two pertains to the Power of Persuasion. In truth, that title appears to have a negative connotation to it. Often, when we think of trying to persuade someone, we think of trickery or fancy rhetoric. Some of us may even think of the Power of Persuasion as the ability to "con." That is not the intention of this book. The ability to effectively persuade someone of something is a necessary component to our lives; especially in parenting, our work, and even during our playtime. However, the nature of this book is to assist you to REACH Presentation Skills so you can be great and inspire; therefore, one must develop sound conversation and persuasion skills. It is the presenter's obligation to his or her audience.

The word *persuasion* is defined as the following: to induce or convince someone to do something or act in some manner. However, as you will read in section two, the Power of Persuasion has a second important component. This component is absolutely necessary when you REACH Presentation Skills, which brings us to section three.

Presentation skills is an area of interest because I become dumbfounded when I learn how much time people spend developing the content of his or her presentation, and then such little time preparing for the actual communication of its content. Interesting, the presenter has certain expectations for the "audience" but does not consider the audience's expectations for the presenter, until the presenter becomes a member of the audience. In other words, the presenter expects the audience to be courteous, quiet, and listen to the presentation. What does the audience expect? This is the question you must ask yourself as you prepare for your presentation. Like most audiences, they expect the presenter to be prepared, informative, accurate, energetic, articulate, interesting and professional. If the presenter is at a loss to any of those fundamentals, he or she will likely lose his or her audience. If the material you are going to present is important, reach your audience by making the material that you so diligently developed, sound important with effective presentation skills.

Although the Power of Conversation and the Power of Persuasion may be perceived to be themes that would be better suited for a sales and marketing seminar, it is important to note that everyday life events bring with it reasons to utilize effective communication skills.

Therefore, everybody should be cognizant of further developing his or her communication skills. God must think this is important; as you will soon learn, certain components of proper communication skills are actually found in the Bible. Moreover, our ancestors have been reading about the importance of effective communication skills. For centuries and throughout continents around the world, these skills have been taught and learned. In short, regardless of what you learn from the latest books on effective communication or regardless of what the lecturers at the latest seminars advocate, many of these lessons and techniques are not cutting-edge; they are not provocative. They have been handed down from generation to generation; they just have fancier titles and price tags on their covers. As I wrote, these techniques may not be new they are, however, the foundation to effective communication. This is the reason I believe it is absolutely necessary to review this topic as you prepare to REACH Presentation Skills so you can be great and inspire.

We should consistently be evaluating and developing not only our children but also ourselves. Using certain techniques from this book can help you in any facet of your life. In truth, we are all salespeople, we are all coaches, we are all teachers and we are all students. Have you ever built a house or a pool, purchased a car or had landscaping done? Have you ever had to explain to your children why a certain behavior is important? Have you ever had to articulate your thoughts and ideas in a professional setting? These are precisely the moments for which we all need to confidently confront people and articulate our thoughts. Whether you are a student, an entrepreneur, a spouse, a parent, a real-estate agent, a doctor, a nurse, or a salesperson, you have to communicate with people. Confidence is key. Consider the right word to be crucial and make the delivery of that word, masterful.

To be able to interact with people in an influential manner, you have to learn how to use communication skills as well as develop appropriate people skills. Developing and improving your abilities to communicate and work with others will take a combination of skills. At this point of the text, you may be thinking to yourself, "I have come far with my abilities to communicate. I don't have to read this book." Good for you. That is confidence. With that said, it is paramount to be objective and learn that there are always areas in our lives that are in need of development. This certainly includes communication skills. Indeed, we communicate everyday, which simply illustrates the importance of improving this fundamental skill. Just as a golfer works assiduously to improve her golf game with the purpose of lowering her score, so must we improve our communication skills with the intent of reducing the amount of words we choose as a means of translating our message.

Some people are able to meet objectives, while others will fall short; so much has to do with delivering a message effectively. This takes time and practice. Particularly when we are presenting to an audience. In short, if you communicate with others, you need to constantly improve your communication and people skills. Consider this point, the Power of Conversation will add value to your life. Moreover, there is so much potential in communication that you will have the ability to, not only help yourself, but also others. So learn, practice, be great and inspire!

Perfect examples of how people skills and communication skills belong, not only in a salesperson's life, but also in all our lives, are examples of successful parenting. It does not take a Ph.D. in psychology to positively influence a child's life. Sometimes it is a car washer with the right parenting skills and the right set of words who can impact lives for generations.

One remarkable story belongs to number forty of the early 1970's Chicago Bears; his name is Gale Sayers. If you are a football fan, you have heard of this exceptional running back and kick-off return man. Gale Sayers is considered to be one of the greatest backs to ever play the game. He was a five time All-Pro and inducted into the Hall of Fame in 1977. When asked who inspired him, his answer was, "A car washer!" This was a person who quit high school and went to work washing cars for a living. He continued this vocation for thirty-five years. This man pleaded with Gale Sayers and repeatedly uttered, "Continue your education, don't quit school and make something of yourself." Who was this man who inspired Gale Sayers so greatly? Gale Sayers' father.

Since I have become a father, I have been awakened to the many similarities of helping both employees and children with their respective development. There is a need for positive and negative reinforcement in both areas of development. Essentially, positive reinforcement is critical in one's development; unfortunately, employers, coaches and parents alike easily underutilize this behavioral modification method. The expectations of a trainee and a child are also not short of its similarities. I asked a series of salespersons and trainees what they desire most from their managers and trainers as well as what they desired least. What follows are the top responses:

☺ What components they find most appealing:
  1. Trust (62%)
  2. Communication skills (21%)
  3. Support (11%)
  4. Coaching (2%)
     (342 respondents)

☹ What set of components they find to be *least* appealing is as follows:
  1. Believing that there is only one way to do something
  2. Viewing representatives as "prototypes"
  3. Lack of objectivity or understanding

Can you assume that these same answers would be consistent if they were asked to a precocious child, in regard to their relationship with their parents? In retrospect, don't you wish your parents had brought you up with the same positive fundamentals? Most of us have the potential to inspire others. Most of us have the ability to shape someone else's life positively or negatively; the choice and responsibility is up to each one of us. Always keep in mind the following: It is more than just knowledge; it is also the application of that knowledge. Without the latter, what good is the former?

So, what are you waiting for? REACH Presentation Skills, be

great and inspire!

PERSEVERANCE

and my

OPPORTUNITIES to grow

Are my

WEAPONS

In

EVERY

REALM of my life!

SECTION ONE

1

SECTION ONE

The Power of Conversation

The

Power

Of

Conversation

"Do not let any unwholesome talk come out of your mouths, but only what is helpful for building others up according to their needs, that it may benefit those who listen."

EPHESIANS 4:29

Are You a Mortal or an Insect?

There were two professors from the university searching for answers. One professor, who seemed to clothe himself in an aura of self-righteousness, searched for cues or information that would support his theories; his name was Mr. Joshua. The other, Mr. McLittle, searched more discretely. One day, they found their views contrasted sharply to one another on a particular subject; therefore, they decided to continue their academic pursuit in a more unorthodox manner. They learned that there was an old yet wise man who lived deep in an Italian forest just outside of Rome. The two professors were informed by some of the town people that this old man's preference was to be left in solitude; however, should anyone have an enchanting question, he was willing to share his knowledge. Of course, as always, there was a price to be paid. A young, eager boy with big, deep green eyes informed the professors, "This eccentric old man prefers his privacy but if he is going to be disturbed, it must be for a challenging and intellectual question. If he considers your visit to be less intellectually stimulating and more of a disturbance, it is rumored he has the ability to change mortals into mere insects! This is the price that must be paid by anyone willing to take the chance." Although the boy's warning caught their attention, they smirked at each other without concern.

"How could that 'legend' be possible?" Mr. Joshua asked Mr. McLittle as both men turned from the boy and walked away laughing.

Soon after the two professors began their journey into the forest, they had to yield to a creek. Already confused and disorientated, they attempted to discern which way they needed to go. It did not take much time to elapse for the debate to culminate into an argument, with each man pointing in opposing directions; consequently, Mr. Joshua decided to go east, Mr. McLittle went west. That moment represented the final moment the two professors would see one another.

Before long, a boy's voice interrupted the serenity that Mr. Joshua was enjoying as he was strolling along the peaceful creek. This agitated him very much because he was in the middle of a thought process. He was toiling with the various ways he could introduce himself and express his ideas to the old, wise man. This feeling of agitation was soon replaced by bewilderment. He thought to himself, "What is a young boy doing out here in the middle of the forest?" The stick in the middle of the path further surprised him. It caused him to trip and fall to the ground in a very ungraceful manner.

He looked like a drunken three hundred pound figure skater tumbling to the ice. As the boy began to chuckle, Mr. Joshua noticed the boy's face; it was familiar. He realized that this was the same boy who informed them about the old man in the forest and the old man's ability to change mortals into insects. "What are..." before he could finish, the boy interrupted him.

"Have you formulated your question for the old, wise man?" The boy continued before Mr. Joshua could answer, "Because, maybe you should ask me first," and then he began to flap his arms as if attempting to fly, "remember...Buzz!"

Mr. Joshua picked himself up from the ground, smirked and responded contemptuously, "How could you possibly help me; you are just a boy?"

"Well, one thing is for sure," the boy exclaimed, "I know enough to step over sticks!" The boy was dramatic with his hand gestures as he emphasized the word "over" and then he covered his mouth as he burst out laughing.

Mr. Joshua responded defensively as he slapped the dirt off the knee of his pants, "I have been teaching runts like you before you were even a thought to your mama. What could I possibly learn from you?" He turned and walked away with his nose high in the air as if designating himself the winner of the debate.

Before long, he heard the boy's voice once again break the silence. "Humor me! What are you planning to ask the old man?"

"Well," whispered Mr. Joshua to himself, "why not, it will be good practice if nothing else."

Once Mr. Joshua began to "open up" and speak, the boy became dumbfounded by Mr. Joshua's sudden change of tone and enthusiasm. The boy saw Mr. Joshua transform from an impatient, ornery, and resolute old man, to a *chattering know-it-all, in a matter of seconds. The boy was reminded of an old wooden house, which gradually burned down. He remembered first noticing the manner in which the flames were captured inside the house searching for more oxygen. Once a large window broke and allowed the oxygen to come in and meet the fire, the flames and temperature increased proportionately. The thick, black, ugly smoke, which accompanied the growing inferno, came pouring out of the broken window. The flames, inevitably, engulfed the house.*

At first, the boy really did not understand what Mr. Joshua was saying because Mr. Joshua was not really speaking to the boy; he was speaking to himself, more or less.

"Mumble, murmur, mumble, murmur, and then I think I will discuss with the old man the importance of proper conversation skills. The importance of having full knowledge of the topics discussed and speaking with conviction so nobody could doubt one's statements and claims. I also believe," continued Mr. Joshua, "the power of persuasion can be mastered by anybody who knows how to talk on and on about a subject so the person being addressed finds himself (or herself) incredibly impressed with the speaker's vast knowledge."

Mr. Joshua continued without taking a breath. After a long period of time, the boy made some considerable attempts to participate in the conversation, however, his words fell upon deaf ears.

"Well boy," said Mr. Joshua after awhile, "what do you think? Will the old man be impressed? Boy. Boy! Boy?"

Mr. Joshua looked all around and was shocked to find he was standing in the middle of the forest talking to himself. "Oh well," whispered Mr. Joshua, "he sure is a strange lad." Suddenly he heard the boy's voice from afar:

"Mr. Joshua, I have one question and one comment for you. My question is, did you ever figure out what your question is going to be for the wise man?" He paused slightly, "My comment is," he said loudly and sarcastically, "my

name is Mercury!"

(Mr. Joshua was never seen or heard from again.)

Moments later, Mr. McLittle felt a slight sting on his leg, just above his right knee. As his hand was about to instinctively swoop down to smash the insect, he consciously hesitated and allowed the bug to fly away. Just as he figured out why he blundered, sudden roaring and obnoxious laughter startled him.

"What's wrong? Are you beginning to believe that 'crazy' legend now?" asked the boy with both hands on his belly while he continued to howl in a taunting manner.

"Well no, I..." Mr. McLittle responded in a humiliated fashion. His humiliation turned into perplexity, which, consequently, made him turn his awkward response into a question, "What are you doing here?"

The boy said, "I often walk here to get away from people. Most people are afraid to come into this forest." Once again he proceeded to flap his arms as if attempting to fly, "Remember...Buzz!"

Mr. McLittle forced a smile to form on his face. The boy continued, "What are you planning to ask the old, wise man?"

Mr. McLittle replied, "Mr. Joshua and I are professors at University State and we are doing some research on the power of conversation and the power of persuasion for a seminar. As we were attempting to design an outline for the program, we found our ideologies were vastly different. We disagreed so often that we decided to continue our research without the use of books. This is the reason we are searching for the old, wise man. By the way, my name is Mr. McLittle, what is your name?"

"Mercury, nice to meet you, again!"

Mr. McLittle asked, "Indeed, you are a precocious young lad; are you named after the Roman god of Eloquence and Cleverness?"

Mercury, with his big, deep green eyes, looked straight into Mr. McLittle's eyes and answered, "Something like that. By the way Mr. McLittle, your right shoelace is untied." He then made another inquiry, "What is your opinion on the subject of the power of conversation and the power of persuasion?"

Mr. McLittle said, as he proceeded to bend down and tie his shoelace, "Essentially, I am of the opinion that in order to be able to persuade someone of something, I must first learn about the person I am attempting to influence. I believe I should speak 'with' this person and not speak 'at' this person. The best way to do this is to allure her into a conversation with something of interest. This will enable me to learn from her what she believes to be important, henceforth, eliminating my guesswork. This technique will also assist me in further understanding that person's opinion, background and way of thinking. Contrary to my colleague's opinion, I do not believe I must talk 'on and on' with the hope that something I say will either impress her or peak her interest. What is your opinion on this topic, Mercury?"

Mercury just smiled and said in an old man's voice, "I agree one hundred percent!"

Mr. McLittle, eyes still fixed on his shoe, immediately dropped his shoelaces before he had the opportunity to tie them while he, simultaneously, looked up at what he thought was going to be the boy, Mercury.

Forgetting why he was on one knee addressing his shoelace, the word "Amazing!" seemed to involuntarily radiate from Mr. McLittle's mouth as he exhaled and gazed in wonderment. "You are Mercury, the Roman god of Eloquence and Cleverness! Are you the old, wise man that lives in this forest who has been foretold?"

Mercury just shook his head up and down as he smiled and seemed to declare his cleverness through his big, deep green and this time, aged eyes. Then Mercury continued to eloquently articulate his thoughts as he bent *down to finish tying Mr. McLittle's untied shoelace.*

"What you are claiming is that sometimes we must remember to press our mute button and listen while we're in a conversation with another or if we are attempting to influence another; I completely agree!" The old, eloquent, and clever Mercury continued, "A good conversation between two people is much like tying this shoelace Mr. McLittle, we are in need of two ends of the shoelace to complete the job, successfully."

The Power of Conversation

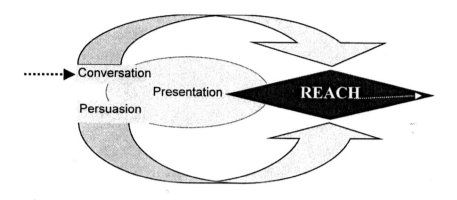

The Power of Conversation must be established before one can improve upon the Power of Persuasion and REACH Presentation Skills. Most people probably don't think much about the importance of or relevance for improving their skill to converse, particularly when they attempt to present. Yet we rely on these skills every-single-day for almost every single situation. Choosing the appropriate word(s) with the appropriate disposition may make all the difference when you are, for example, attempting to convince your child the importance of not smoking cigarettes or, for that matter, the importance of living a life full of meaning. You should put as much preparation into these conversations as you would if you were about to discuss an issue with your supervisor, a client or as you would for a job interview. If you are not preparing before any important conversation, you are failing to meet your potential and you will likely be unable to make a maximum impact. You are, essentially, more likely to fail with the *purpose* of the conversation.

Think about how much time most of us spend grooming ourselves, and dressing appropriately with the intent of a proper presentation. Every-single-day, we are trying to find the right clothing to wear for the right situation. We try to get our hair, our nails, and our face just right. We groom, primp, and spruce up ourselves to perfection. This involves a lot of effort and, quite frankly, should. In most anything we do, our presentation to the world is important. This importance is the reason we should put forth such endeavors. What about our verbal presentation? Why do we not place as much emphasis on our presentation skills as we do with our physical appearance?

Our innate ability to learn permits us to improve upon any skill we choose. There is no better way to become more skilled in writing, basketball, martial arts, golf, reading, playing an instrument or improving on any other skill for that matter that should interest you, then by learning how to improve upon those skills. Once you learn how to improve, the next step is to execute, routinely, appropriate measures. This most certainly applies to our verbal skills; thus, the Power of Conversation.

We must be aware of the importance of grooming our communication skills just as we are aware of the importance of maintaining our overall physical appearance. Just as it is important to have polished shoes to go with a nice suit, we must stress the importance of sounding polished when we communicate. After all, our family, friends, colleagues and customers will respond to our words and the way in which we choose to express those words. Ask yourself, "How is my language being perceived?" When was the last time you took the time to practice and, thus, work toward improving your communication skills? Yes, it is important to "dress for success" however it is equally important to *speak* for success. French may be the "language of love," however proper grammar is the language for success. In short, if your overall presentation is important to you, your communication skills should be important to you. After all, it is a function of your overall appearance.

DISCRETION (not grease) "IS THE WORD, IS THE WORD, IS THE WORD"

One word, or a series of words assembled together, can sound as poetic as the sounds of nightfall in Venice, as your lover and you tenderly glide through its canals with the whispers and songs of your personal gondolier (how lovely!). With that said, one word, or series of words assembled together, can also sound as foul and repudiating as the sound of someone scratching and scraping all ten of his or her fingernails against a chalk-board, from one end to the other, with the sole intent of creating a bone agitating, teeth grating noise (how dreadful!).

Most of us have considerable judgment and that judgment allows us to choose words with discretion. The words you choose to articulate, most certainly represent the person you are, just as your choice of clothing represent you. People will perceive you in a certain light when they listen to you speak. Be aware that this is a fact. Be aware that this fact breeds discretion. Be aware that this discretion is your ability to choose your language, thereby making your language your choice, thus, your responsibility. Should you not believe that improving your communication skills is important, consider the reason that exceeds your self-interest; consider your children. Fortunately, it is easy to deliver a word, or a series of words, that will brighten a child's day. Unfortunately, it is easier to deliver a word, or a series of words, that will darken a child's life. A word is a potent instrument for child rearing and that reality must command accountability.

With regard to accountability, in corporate America, you will be fired from your job so quickly for choosing one wrong word, that you'll hear an explosion. That explosion will be due to the human resource department moving at super-sonic speed, thereby breaking the sound barrier, as they feverishly gather the legal documents that are required for your removal from the company. One word can be so hurtful. You don't have to go any further than Don Imas as proof of the consequences that manifest as a result of an inappropriate phrase or word. He was a national broadcaster who sparked controversy in 2007 when he called a group of female basketball players "Hoes." He lost his job along with his dignity. People perceived him differently and his world was turned upside-down minutes after that badly chosen word came from his mouth.

Regarding a hurtful word, or series of words, what kind of guardian does a child have to protect himself or herself? As previously mentioned, the essence to the Power of Conversation in this book is to improve your communication skills so you will be capable to REACH Presentation Skills. This skill will also help you improve your personal relationships. This applies to any relationship within your personal "world," however, none as critical as the relationship between a child and you. Don't disappoint the future by using disparaging words that are directed at your children; you will, subsequently, be limiting your children's potential. It is a parent, guardian, or teacher's obligation to choose, with discretion, appropriate language. Life is a relay race and you will hand a baton to your children as they grow into young adults and seek their independence. Hand them encouragement as they make their strides. The better skilled and mindful you are with the words you choose, the more likely you, and the people within your world, will realize success.

What follows are just a few examples of how you can deliver, fundamentally, the same message, however with a softer, less abrasive and less harmful tone:

Harsh and abrasive language	Appropriate language
⇒ "I need to steal business from my competitor!"	⇒ "I need to increase market-share."
⇒ "We need to 'target' customers."	⇒ "We need to assist our customers with their needs."
⇒ "I feel like 'crap!'"	⇒ "I do not feel well."
⇒ "When it comes to math, you are really stupid!"	⇒ "Your science class is your strength, however, we need to focus a little more attention on your math skills."
⇒ "I don't got nothin'."	⇒ "I do not have anything."
⇒ "I am mad at you again! Why do you always make me mad."	⇒ "I am upset with you due to your inappropriate behavior!"

You are going to have to converse with people when you REACH Presentation Skills, thus, converse effectively. It should come as little surprise to anyone reading these words that as one moves away from an educational environment and toward a work environment, one's exposure to learning the details and workings of the English language become less routine and, therefore, limited. As a result, one is more likely to fail to recall certain rules of communication, whether verbal, written or otherwise. Another issue is that, to a degree, society has become more tolerant, or relaxed, with the rules of communication, as it compares to generations past. This emerging tolerance is creating an ever-growing dichotomy between those who speak well versus those who don't. That gap is as wide as those who care versus those who don't; be among the former. Avoid walking into the trap of indifference. Take steps to ensure that your language is viewed receptively among those to whom you speak, especially if you want people to respond favorably to your words.

Perhaps you don't consider your work environment or lifestyle, areas in which proper grammar is necessary. This may or may not be true today. The fact is, as we get older, our lifestyles, careers and friends change. A situation that is not important today may be paramount tomorrow. For example, planning for retirement. When we are young, we don't consider the importance of allocating a large percentage of our money toward a retirement plan. We prefer to spend our money on cars, friends, freedom and vacations. As we get older, our lifestyle and priorities change and we sometimes wish that we invested earlier. The earlier we start planning and investing for our future, the better prepared we are when the time comes. The same can be said regarding preparing yourself with proper communication skills. When you are young, slang is more acceptable and speaking properly is not important. As you get older, however, your situation changes and having the ability to properly communicate with your family, friends and peers will likely be more important. If you plan while you are young by being, not only cognizant, but also diligent, of improving your skills routinely, just as you would invest a percentage of your pay routinely, you will subtly improve your communication skills and be prepared when the time comes.

It is for these reasons that it is important to take action. Take some refresher English courses, review books with a focus on grammar, read more frequently, practice, and be aware of the words you choose. Use discretion, especially when it really counts. When it comes to the people in your world, including personally or professionally, it should always count. In essence, be mindful and remember, 'Discretion' (not grease) is the word, is the word, is the word.

IS ANYBODY LISTENING?

> *He who answers a matter before he*
> *hears it,*
> *It is folly and shame to him.*
> Proverbs 18:13

"We have two ears and one mouth…use them proportionately!"

There are few things more obnoxious than having a discussion with a "know-it-all" and having that know-it-all not allow others to contribute a verse. A person who talks indiscriminately, without any concern for the other person's viewpoint, is lacking impartiality, is selfish and is presumptuous. The speaker lacks impartiality because he is not trying to learn anything from the person with whom he is conversing. Moreover, the speaker is selfish because he is dominating the conversation and finally, he is presumptuous because he is presuming the recipient is captivated by his every last word. To quote the Scarecrow from the 1939 film, *The Wizard of Oz*, "People without brains do a lot of talking, don't they?" You may recall that that was the question the Scarecrow posed to Dorothy after Dorothy commented to him that he must have a brain because he is able to talk. With that said, shouldn't a conversation be more like a tennis match (going back and forth) and less like a one-person racquetball game (one person continuously banging "words" against a wall)?

The actual state of the matter is that if you are a person who is in the habit of monopolizing a conversation, the people you are addressing will, more than likely, become bored of your words. Moreover, because this behavior developed into a habit, you will likely become infamous for this behavior and, consequently, people will avoid engaging you. This statement is not a simple embellishment. Most will agree that they do not like to speak to people with narrow-minded views. As a former sales trainer, I have frequently seen this error in judgment. Additionally, in terms of social skills and communication skills, I have become aware of the way people behave, respond and react to one another, as they exchange words. This is an important function of my job as a sales trainer, as a salesperson and certainly a father and a husband. For example, to be able to establish a rapport with a potential client is an absolute must. How is this endeavor accomplished? It is accomplished by way of effective communication skills; the ability to converse, intelligently, sincerely, and *sensitively*.

I underscore the word sensitively because we must *sense* how the person, with whom we are speaking, is receiving our message. In short, does the recipient consider the articulation of my thoughts, stimulating? Or, does she find my vocalization long-winded or loquacious? When the latter scenario occurs, I wish the person speaking to me were 7,926 miles away from me (This is the equatorial diameter of the Earth thus, the farthest one human can get from another human on Earth.) Forget the cliché that one must have "the gift of gab" to be a successful speaker, conversationalist or salesperson. What about the gift to listen? The chances are, you probably have been acquainted with plenty of people who can gab, and gab, and gab but how many people have you encountered who have the unique gift to listen?

The parable about the two professors is a fine example of how important it is for us to work toward the Power of Conversation before we can use the Power of Persuasion and ultimately REACH Presentation Skills. Mr. Joshua was convinced he was full of knowledge. In fact, that was how he wanted to be perceived because he believed it would make him more credible. As a consequence, Mercury, the Roman god of Eloquence and Cleverness, perceived Mr. Joshua as condescending. Mr. Joshua believed his words were full of intrigue; as it turned out, his words were full of something all together different. What he lacked was impartiality, sensitivity and the unique skill to listen. For example, he believed he could not learn "from a mere boy!" therefore, Mercury's perception of Mr. Joshua was the following: he was patronizing, pompous, and insensitive. Consequently, Mr. Joshua lost the interest of the person he was addressing. He was not only irritating to listen to, his mere presence was irritating; much like an insect flying around one's head as it creates, while in flight, that exasperating sound as its microscopic wings mechanically flutter back and forth, seemingly hundreds of times per second, inches from your unprotected ears.

Conversely, Mr. McLittle had the appropriate skills of an interesting conversationalist. He understood the importance of bringing Mercury into the conversation by way of asking him his opinion on the said topic. He also was aware of the importance of truly listening to Mercury's response so he could, not only learn from him, but also better understand him. He recognized the importance of a mutual introduction with the purpose of each person learning the other's name. A stranger seems less strange when you learn his name. As my good friend, Tim Culver, once said during his eulogy the day his loving father passed away:

> "Whenever a stranger met my father, they would part one another as friends."

Contrary to many a person's opinion, there is nothing wrong with making friends or acquaintances. There is a whole world of wealth out there, as long as you consider friendship valuable. With that said, think how much knowledge can be gained if you learn to open up to people and remain impartial. Most people have a talent they are willing to share; all you need to do is listen.

I knew of a professional driver who owned a limousine service. Every day or night, she would pick up her customers and drop them off at their destination. She would go from point A to point B and then start all over again with another customer. Some might believe this to be a boring way to make a living. Not her, she once told me, "I love my job. I get to drive around town with all my friends." This outlook on life was her good nature coming through for all of her clients to experience. She clearly has optimism running through her veins. She is also intelligent and demonstrates that intelligence to her clients. She once told me, "Another benefit to driving various people around all day is I get to listen and learn from them. I could have paid a group of consultants a million dollars for what I have learned for free; just because I listen."

Mr. McLittle, from the above parable, realized there is always something to be gained when he listens and, if he approaches people with this impartiality, he will continue to, not only learn and grow as an individual, he will also make others feel their opinion is important to him. Consequently, Mr. McLittle learned who the boy truly was (the Roman god of Eloquence and Cleverness). As it happened, the art of language was Mercury's core competency. Once Mr. McLittle learned who Mercury was and what Mercury's hidden talents were, i.e., the gift to speak eloquently and the gift to be clever or quick-witted, he was able to continue learning from him. Mr. McLittle was able to succeed because of his ability to converse effectively and he, ultimately, was able to learn what Mercury's opinion was on the topic of conversation and persuasion.

After all, wasn't that the main purpose of the two professors' journey into the Forest?

> *A word fitly spoken is like apples of gold*
> *In settings of silver*
> Proverbs 25:11

Proverbs 25:11 sums up the importance of choosing the right word(s) and making the delivery of those word(s) masterful. At times you will hear the words that people select to be appropriate, well thought out, intelligent and prepared because they are relevant to, and expand on, the conversation. Those are the times that "a word fitly spoken is like apples of gold in settings of silver." Those are the times that the words chosen become precious because they have the ability to create inspiration. If words are inappropriate to the conversation, then they simply don't fit. You might as well be whispering in the dark because nobody is really listening to you in an inspirational fashion. In fact, on the contrary, they might hear your ill-advised words, become offended, and react in a manner of discord. To REACH Presentation Skills, you must make your words fit the moment; therefore, chose your words judiciously and deliver those words, masterfully.

Recommended methods to improving your listening skills: While the person is speaking, ask yourself the following simple questions:

⇒ Listen attentively and ask yourself, what is his or her point?
⇒ Is his or her point logical?
⇒ Do you agree with his or her point-of-view? If not, what is your reasoning?
⇒ Regardless of whether or not you agree with the view, is the view logical?
⇒ How can you expand on his or her views?
⇒ What is his or her background and why does he or she view it that way?
⇒ What? Where? How? Why? Who?

The Rules of Communiqué

It is difficult to give a set of concrete rules as to how to develop and improve on communication skills because it is not: Do step 'a' then go to step 'b' and then 'c'. If you attempt to follow an algorithm, it will be obvious to the person to whom you are speaking; essentially, you will sound too mechanical. You have to learn the techniques while incorporating your own style. Your style is what comes natural to you. Your style in this lesson is your personality.

Learning new communication skills is much like a dancer learning new choreography. First, the dancer learns the technique and mechanics of the choreography. After a certain amount of practice, the choreography becomes natural to the dancer. This is when skilled dancers incorporate their own style into the dance and make the dance extraordinary. "It is not the dance that makes the dancer; it is the dancer who makes the dance." The same is true with conversationalist. It is not necessarily the context of the conversation that makes the conversationalist; it is the conversationalist who makes the conversation. Finally, it is not the context of the presentation that makes the presenter, but the presenter who makes the presentation. Hence, the first rule: Learn new skills and improve upon those skills but do so by keeping your own original style. You are not you without you.

To illustrate, there was a new representative who learned all she could learn about the potential client who she was preparing to visit. This is a very intelligent step to take; it is called a "pre-call" plan. In a sense, she was preparing for an important conversation. The problem was, once she got in front of the client, she began to regurgitate most of the client's personal information that she had recently learned. She failed to stay focused on her purpose. She began to mechanically question the customer as if she had been calling on him for years; i.e., "So how is your daughter, Sara?" He responded. "How is your dog, Buddy?" He responded. "Have you been able to go out on the boat lately?" He took a deep breath and then responded. "How is your son doing at Florida State University?" He responded, curtly.

While she was in training, she learned the important technique of pre-call planning. She attempted to implement this skill in her first appointment with a customer she had never met. Her intent was two-fold: to establish a rapport and to sell her product. Her efforts on both items proved futile because she failed to stay true to herself. She had this wonderful persona but she was unable to show it because she was anxious and became immersed in technique. In short, she used a new technique but she sacrificed her natural style. As you could imagine, the customer found the scenario to be quite peculiar. He curtailed the appointment before the over zealous salesperson could begin discussing her product.

Discussing the product was the purpose of being in front of the customer in the first place. The point is, it is not simply learning new techniques that will assist you in improving your conversation skills. It is also your ability to rely on your instincts. You have to trust yourself. It is about learning who you are and having the confidence in the person you have become while you are engaged with another. This is an additional reason it is imperative to be a person of integrity and moral character. You should be confident in allowing others to get to know you. This will fortify a mutual trust.

With that said, as you work to improve your listening skills, it is not only important to implement technique, it is also important to apply your personal signature to those techniques. Indeed, this is not a provocative idea but is certainly worthy of another mention. Regardless of what skill you work to develop, you first learn the mechanics of that skill. Once your body gets familiar with the mechanics, after a certain amount of repetition, the movements become automatic. As previously communicated, this is precisely the time your style is added. Artists can always determine when they finally become confident with an illustrative technique; the technique, which initially felt clumsy, subtly becomes comfortable. They learn how to use light with imagery and then distinguish themselves from other artists by applying their unique signature patterns to the learned techniques. It is at that moment they invite their style to join them and contribute to their work. This keen ability is what enables them to become skilled artists. This is true in any art form; including the art of conversation, persuasion and presentation. For all intents and purposes, each is an art within itself.

You must also experiment and learn what works and what does not work out in the world. Improving those skills with your natural style will help you REACH Presentation Skills and become inspirational. Parenthetically, for further development, I recommend reading Stephen R. Covey's *The 7 Habits of Highly Effective People*. One valuable lesson you will read about in this book is the importance of being yourself during a conversation. He also brings to light the significance of being a person of integrity as you converse with others. Mr. Covey is a proponent of the following:

"The most important ingredient we put into any relationship is not what we say or what we do, but what we are. And if our words and our actions come from superficial human relations techniques rather than from our own inner core, others will sense that duplicity. We simply won't be able to create and sustain the foundation necessary for effective interdependence.

"The techniques and skills that really make a difference in human interaction are the ones that almost naturally flow from a truly independent character. So the place to begin building any relationship is inside ourselves, inside our circle of influence, our own character."[1]

Be mindful of your inner core as you work on improving your conversation skills and consider every conversation as an opportunity to grow. Likewise, the more you practice certain techniques, the more comfortable you will be, thus, you will appear more sincere. This will, more than likely, motivate the person, to whom you are speaking, to relax and be willing to open up to you. Once you gain the trust of that person, you'll find that the dialogue will flow naturally. The more natural the conversation, the more natural you will become and that will allow you to be you. Subsequently, you'll be in a better position to achieve your mission.

The Power of Understanding

> *Happy is the man who finds wisdom, and*
> *the man who gains understanding;*
> *For her proceeds are better than the*
> *profits of silver,*
> *And her gain than fine gold.*
> Proverbs 3:13-14

Proverbs 3:13-14 refers to the value of wisdom and understanding. So much wisdom can be found when one gains understanding. If the conversation is important, you should make it a priority to truly understand what the other person is saying and feeling. Understanding should be viewed as a skill for which we all are in need of improvement. The Power of Understanding can easily be underutilized and its importance easily underestimated. Developing an understanding will help you gain greater insight into a topic and the mindset of another.

For example, if an employee tells you that he has been up all night with his new born baby and that working a twelve-hour shift will be difficult, you are more inclined to be empathetic and make concessions if you have children of your own than if you are single and never had to stay up all night with a crying baby in the past. It is only natural to better understand something when you have gone through it yourself. We all understand sleep deprivation, hunger, pain and sickness because we have all experienced these human discomforts. We understand via empathy and so we are more prepared to discuss them intelligently and make better decisions regarding such physical stresses.

We become shortsighted, however, when we have little or no experience in something. It becomes much more difficult to understand the things or events that we have not personally gone through. For example, not everybody understands how difficult it is to quit smoking cigarettes. You can hear about it from someone going through it, but if you haven't had to rip the addiction's mighty grip from your very existence, you couldn't understand the true nature of the fight. It would take a lot of skill for you to listen and learn from the one who is trying to explain the battle that a smoker has to experience when he or she decides to quit, if you haven't gone through this battle yourself. As one who never smoked cigarettes, it is easy for me to say, "Just quit!" The truth is, this type of insensitive comment isn't fair and it is made due to a lack of understanding. To learn to understand another is a skill, which is as important as any other skill, as you work to improve upon your conversation skills and REACH Presentation Skills.

Should you be interested in taking your conversation skills to a higher level, I also recommend you read a book titled *Difficult Conversations* by Stone, Patton and Heen. This is an in-depth view of the importance of accepting that you are not likely to truly understand another person's feelings, values, history and ever changing emotions which shape that person's views and interpretation of a topic, argument or opinion. However, you can attempt to make large strides to further learn from that person. Why is that so important to note? As you attempt to learn to understand the decision-making process, background and values of the person with whom you are speaking, you will have a greater probability of understanding that person's point-of-view. Moreover, the more you understand a person's point-of-view and why they have formed an opinion about a specific topic, the easier it is to reach some type of agreement or common ground. For example, the more you understand someone's values, the more you are likely to understand his or her decision-making process. With that said, the more you understand your values, the better you will understand yourself and your decision-making process.

Difficult Conversations underscores the importance of remaining open to another's point-of-view. You must learn to be objective when you are conversing with and/or attempting to persuade someone of something. For example, while you were in the middle of a frustrating conversation with someone in the past, how often have you asked yourself the following question?

"Why doesn't he see it my way? My view is so logical and his is so irrational. Clearly I am in the right!"

If the previously mentioned are your thoughts while the other person is speaking, you are not really listening to that person or attempting to understand that person. In its stead, you are merely waiting for him to finish speaking so you can speak. This action will more than likely derail you from accomplishing your purpose or goal. Remember the importance of always remaining focused on the purpose of the conversation. The purpose (or point) of the conversation is not to win a debate and prove you are intellectually superior. The purpose is the reason for the conversation. If you are acting and reacting with the sole intent of winning a debate, the person, to whom you are speaking, will get frustrated with your lack of concern, lack of feelings, lack of impartiality and lack of respect for his or her point-of-view. If you really want to improve on your conversation and persuasive skills, practice being impartial while, at the same time, remaining focused on the purpose of the discussion. Indeed, I will be the first to admit that trying to remain impartial is no easy task especially when the conversation becomes emotional. However, to try to understand someone, you have to learn to remain balanced.

In addition, make a serious effort to improve on your listening skills (as discussed above). Your listening skills will keep you balanced in the conversation. It is vital to comprehend one simple fact: listening is a teammate, and not a competitor, of speaking during a conversational event. So, consider every conversation as an event while speaking with someone else. First start by practicing one of the most important and perhaps less sought after skills: the skill of listening. Second, while you are listening, try to really understand the person to whom you are speaking. To assist you with this endeavor, ask yourself the following two questions:

> ⇒ I wonder why she understands that condition in that fashion?
> ⇒ What values, history or set of circumstances is she drawing from to make her form that conclusion or view?

If you can learn to do that successfully, you are more likely to understand that person's reasoning. You are that much closer to meeting common ground. You are that much closer to accomplishing your purpose of the conversation. Keep in mind that to successfully persuade someone does not necessarily mean you have to be declared the winner of the debate. It means you met your goal. It also means that you learned something of value. The funny thing about knowing that you are right is that if "right" came in colors, it would come in a variety of achromatic colors. At times it would be black or white; but often it would show itself in various shades of gray.

What follows is an illustration of the Power of Understanding

Dr. Phil is a psychologist who has his own talk show. During one episode, he interviewed a woman who was in the habit of being extremely rude to the wait staff at various restaurants. While interacting with such personnel, her zone of tolerance was quite narrow. In fact, one night she was filmed yelling and belittling the wait staff at a particular restaurant. Her husband was embarrassed to say that this behavior of hers is common. During her interview, she told Dr. Phil that she believed "all the wait-staff had to do was fetch some glasses of water and take orders. How difficult is that?" She said that she couldn't understand how a waiter could make mistakes because the job is so one-dimensional. In short, she thought they were inept. That was until Dr. Phil had her "walk in their shoes." She agreed to wait on tables at a restaurant and learn for herself the nuances of the job. Dr. Phil and his crew filmed her experience.

What did she learn? If you ever waited on tables, you likely have an idea. In terms of her success as a waitress, she had only one. She successfully learned how difficult it is to be a waitress. She made more mistakes than she had tables to wait on. In fact, her performance was so poor that the tables were waiting on her! While the norm at this restaurant is to service approximately twenty to thirty tables a night, she only serviced three. She admitted to Dr. Phil that after her poor experience as a waitress, she was sorry she ever disrespected waiters and waitresses in the past. She said she would certainly have much more tolerance and much more understanding (empathy) in the future. It was as if she was sleeping all these years and now, due to her experience, she has been awoken. Suddenly, waiters and waitresses are hard working, intelligent, service oriented people who are trying to earn a living.

She learned this because she was put in the position to learn more about the people she was harshly judging. Prior to her experience as a waitress, she was assuming one thing about a group of people and, subsequently, passing judgment on those people. After her enlightenment, when she learned enough to the degree that she no longer has to make anymore assumptions about the task of serving customers, she now understands this group of people and respects them for their efforts. Interestingly, it was at that point, when she finally understood them, that she then found respect for them and for their work. Consequently, she no longer ridiculed a wait staff nor will she ridicule them in the future. It was at that point of the interview when the woman finally began to sound intelligent. It was the point when she was better able to articulate the details of a wait staff's duties. "Happy is the man who finds wisdom, and the man who gains understanding; for her proceeds are better than the profits of silver, and her gain than fine gold" (Proverbs 3:13-14). Ah, the Power of Understanding!

Another *FREAKY* Illustration

I took my daughter to see a Disney film titled *Freaky Friday*. When I saw the movie I immediately thought of the book I mentioned above, *Difficult Conversations*. The premise of the movie is how living in another person's shoes will make you understand that person's decision-making process. In the movie, Jamie Lee Curtis is a middle-aged, full-time successful psychologist, who is busy rearing her two children: a ten-year-old son and a sixteen-year-old daughter. In the beginning of the movie, the teenage daughter resisted the mother like a big oak tree standing steadfast in the middle of an open field against a physically powerful windstorm. No matter what was said, there was a disagreement to follow. As for the mother, she was also to blame; she was oblivious to her daughter's needs.

Throughout the film, their relationship was less than favorable because they did not understand one another. As the film reached its conclusion, however, the mother-daughter duo would live happily-ever-after. What is most relevant to this section of The Power of Understanding is what had occurred between the beginning and ending of the movie that brought them both together. That relevance may be summed up with three simple words: understanding through empathy.

One morning, the daughter woke up in her mother's body and the mother in her daughter's body. As the film progressed, each learned what it was like to literally walk in the other woman's shoes. They understood each other's "worlds" (metaphorically speaking), reasoning, and decision-making process. That new, profound understanding, for which they had learned as a result of living the other's life, is what brought them together in the end. They understood each other completely, thus they were more willing to meet mutual ground on issues. What a great gift.

The Power of Understanding has the potential to help bring metaphorical worlds together, one conversation at a time. Think about how often something occurred in your life that no one else understood. You knew the situation but the outcome got you into trouble. No matter how much you tried to explain your point-of-view, no one understood. No one but you understood the steps that were out of your control, however, someone else put their own steps together in their own head and the steps lead right to you. How frustrating is that? Your interactions with those people would have been much more productive, if only they were more understanding to the way you understood the circumstances.

To illustrate, one freaky Friday of your own, you were driving home from work and the drive ended with you smashing and destroying some beautiful ceramic statues that were artistically organized on the side of someone's driveway. In the owner's mind, you were not only responsible for the destruction of his property, you were also an idiot! That was what he understood because that was his perception. Your understanding of the unfortunate event that lead to this final outcome was much different. You were driving cautiously and within the speed limit when, suddenly, out of nowhere, another car came barreling out of a parking lot. Although too late, he finally saw you, panicked and proceeded to slam on his brakes. As a result, he stopped halfway into the street leaving you with few options. You instinctively reacted and successfully avoided driving into the side of this person's car. Consequently, you skidded around the car and unavoidably smashed into the ceramic statues. It was at that point, the person, who you skillfully swerved around and spared, drove away. This left only you to blame because no one else saw this driver barreling out of a parking lot and creating the incident.

You can see how the Power of Understanding is important to you when you are desperately attempting to convince someone of something. Therefore, try to see why it is important for you to attempt to understand others, as you want others to try to understand you. Quite often, people believe they have truth on their side and, therefore, justify their actions or perceptions. The issue with truth is its assortment of interpretations. If you can make a habit of considering this valid point and, therefore, the importance of developing the skill of understanding, you will improve upon a skill few have mastered or even considered. Broaden your scope and you will see more of the world.

Do Your Significant Other and You Understand One Another?

Let's find out: A wife and a husband are sitting next to one another in an airplane. The husband is enthusiastically pecking away on his laptop. He is truly oblivious to anything outside of his laptop screen and that indefatigable blinking cursor. It is as if he has entered a new continuum. Suddenly, as if awoken from a dream, he feels a nudge. He realizes it is his wife seeking his attention. She begins to read to him a paragraph from her book. Moments later, he says to her, "Can you read that again, I was not listening." This upsets her. She repeats the paragraph, however, this time she reads curtly. What just happened? Moments ago, they were both fine. In a matter of seconds, she becomes upset with him because she thinks he is indifferent and should have listened to her from the beginning. Subsequently, he gets upset with her because he noticed her state of irritation. What happened versus what could have happened? Let us take a peek into her and his minds, shall we?

The wife's feelings and thoughts were:

"I'd like to share this paragraph with him because it makes for interesting conversation. It allows me to express, in words, how I feel about this topic. He should care enough to drop what he is doing and listen to me. He has been working on his laptop, uninterrupted, for over an hour. I don't do this all the time. It was only one paragraph and it would have taken only twenty seconds of his time."

The husband's feelings and thoughts were:

"I wish she could understand that I was right in the middle of a thought. I was typing this thought down because I had the right sequence of words in my head. If I stopped typing at that moment and listened to her read the paragraph, I feared I would have lost the word order. She could easily just read that paragraph again. It is there in front of her. If it is so important, what is the big deal? I was vigorously trying to finish typing my idea so I would be

able to give her my undivided attention. It literally took me only twenty more seconds to finish typing my thought."

Does the previous scenario have a familiar storyline? If both wife and husband could better understand each of the previously stated thought processes, each would appreciate the other's feelings and reasoning. This would more than likely lead to common ground and mutual understanding. Both thoughts are reasonable and if each could truly understand and appreciate the other's feelings and thoughts, their communication at that moment would be vastly improved. Admittedly, this is much easier to write than it is to implement because it takes a lot of patience and understanding. You have to ask yourself if the nature of the relationship or situation is worth the effort.

To sum up, is "understanding" a valuable component to communication? Well, corporate America seems to think so. Human resource departments across America have initiated a "diversity" policy within their respective multi-billion dollar companies. The goal is to hire and promote people of various genders, customs and ethnicities. The theory is that the more diverse the employees are and the more the company is influenced by those diversities, the stronger the company will become. The reasoning is that the different backgrounds that people bring to a company from all around the world will create different perspectives, ideas and understandings to issues and business acumen. If, for example, an executive hires someone with the same gender, background and experiences that she has, there may be a limitation in both problem solving capabilities as well as creative thinking. If, however, an executive hires someone whose gender or background is completely different than his or hers, the executive may learn to understand issues differently via interactions with that person. They will learn from one another how to more effectively execute plans and manage their business due to an expansion of their overall points-of-view.

My opinion on this topic is that the more you get to understand someone who is very different than you, the more you realize your similarities. Fascinatingly, as you get to know someone who has the same background, interests and culture that you have, you begin to understand just how very different you are to one another. In truth, diversity should not be about skin, religion or culture; it is simply when one "metaphorical" world (the people, places and things that make up each of our individual life) touch another metaphorical world and both worlds are open to learning from and understanding one another. You have to consider that the trouble with truth is its many varieties. This is the Power of Understanding, which is a power that can enable a wealth of possibilities by broadening one's view. For this subject, it will help you improve your conversation skills and you will ultimately be able to REACH Presentation Skills inspirationally.

Get The Point?

Needles are a brilliant invention. Sure, they are small and seem to hold little relative value in our lives. If you happen to notice one in a carpet, you will most likely pick it up and throw it in the trash so no one would step on it. They are virtually worthless. At least we act as if this is true. In all actuality, we probably never think much about a needle until, of course, we are in need of one. When we do find we are in need of a needle, we appreciate it for its wonderful features. Try stitching two materials together without a needle; it can't be done. One feature that makes the needle such a valuable tool to a seamstress is its end. It has a sharp and therefore useful *point*. If you use the tool properly, you will effectively utilize the point and create something of value. The needle can be quite productive. If you disagree, look in your closet and try to find one stitch of clothing that has not been exposed to a needle. You have to *love* the needle!

A needle, at times, is not always so glorious. If you have ever stuck your finger or hand with the point of a needle, you will literally and figuratively know first hand to what I am referring. It is painful. First you puncture your skin and then you anxiously anticipate the blood to come trickling out. Before you know it, you have bloodstains on your garment and pain is soon to follow. These are the times when a point of a needle can be quite destructive. You have to *hate* the needle!

You get the *point*? Participating in a productive conversation not only involves your personality, discretion of words, the ability to listen and be understanding, it is also important to remain focused on the point (or purpose) of the conversation. What you do with that point can either make the conversation valuable and therefore, productive, or it can make the conversation painful and therefore, destructive. The point can make a conversation one you have to love or one you have to hate. So, what is the point?

Ask yourself: What is the point or purpose of the conversation?

Every intelligent conversation has a purpose (or a point). Don't think of every discussion as a debate you have to win. Consider your purpose. Consider your purpose before you begin your discussion and try to remain focused on that purpose. If you are not focused on your purpose and you are not listening to the other person's reasoning, you will likely not meet common ground. You will potentially lose your focus. That can lead to a loss of credibility, wordy dialogue, or worse yet, you may find yourself falling short of your objective.

Let's address a scenario for which I was witness to while I was with a trainee. That particular trainee was in front of her new prospect with the objective of persuading him that our product is better than the competitor's product. She started discussing some of the features of our product. This is very good technical selling. The problem was, before she began discussing the benefits of those features (elaboration of "features and benefits" are in the chapter that follows: The Power of Persuasion) she began talking about her vacation. She lost her train of thought and got sidetracked. Eventually, the prospect tried to get her to go back and present the benefits of the product, however to no avail; she continued discussing her vacation. She lost her focus and altered her direction away from her purpose, which ultimately was to sell her product. No sale! The *point* is, don't let your point get lost in a lexicon of irrelevant words. Once that happens, trying to recover it is much like searching for a needle in a haystack.

From BEAST to BEAUTY

In Disney's *Beauty and the Beast*, the Beast was truly a repugnant looking character. People were shaken by his physical appearance and nasty disposition. In short, he lacked popular appeal and preferred a life of isolation. The question is, was he that horrific or was it simply that people didn't know how to communicate with him?

The answer is that it was the fault of all parties involved. People did not know how to speak to or interact with him because they didn't understand him and he was intimidating. The Beast certainly contributed to the problem because it was he who was so unfriendly and unapproachable. If you read that previous sentence again, I imagine that would describe most strangers as we assess them before we actually attempt to speak with them. People we don't know usually don't appear to be amicable. To many people, it is intimidating to approach and try to communicate with someone they have never met; particularly if it is a potential customer. You become somewhat vulnerable when you are the one attempting to make "first contact." So, what should we do? Should we avoid him at any cost because we fear him as many of the characters in *Beauty and the Beast* avoided and feared the Beast?

Absolutely not! Learn a lesson from the main character, Bell, and utilize your conversation skills to "soften" him up. Once Bell understood the Beast, she got to know him and they learned to trust one another. In the end, the Beast went from a Beastly looking character to a handsome and warm man. In the end, she was able to turn him into the appealing person he really was inside. You can mimic Bell's success by simply communicating more effectively.

The Power of Conversation: Summary

What follows is a summary of techniques, with some additional tips, for this Power of Conversation section. Some of the tips may appear obvious, however, they are certainly underutilized techniques that are important to, not only trainers and salespersons, but also parents, spouses and anyone else attempting to communicate effectively with another. If you can consistently learn to use these skills, you will learn how to transform many "Beasts" into Beauties. The one caveat is, not all beasts will transform. Sometime a beast on the outside is a beast in the inside. Fortunately, the manifestation of the latter is much less frequent than the former. You just have to try. So, what are you waiting for? Be great and inspire as you REACH Presentation Skills.

The Power of Conversation

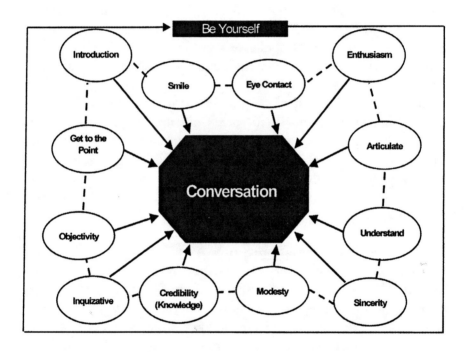

(1) Be Yourself

There is a reason that this heading encompasses each item within the model illustrated above. As each item is important individually, you have to link each individual item together, but you must do so by keeping true to yourself. If you complete each item but do so by failing to incorporate your own personality, you will simply fail. The only way to make this model work is by putting you at its forefront. Trust your personality; trust yourself as you REACH Presentation Skills.

(2) Introduce yourself in a non-threatening and gracious manner

Have you ever noticed how defensive many people are, regardless of whether they are in a public or private domain? Many people never seem to let their guard down. Many people are rude, or appear to be rude, simply because they are "on alert!" Many people do not like the vulnerability associated with being the first to extend a hand with the intention of offering a welcoming handshake. What can you do about it? Be the first to extend your hand and graciously introduce yourself. You will find that the people who have their guard up will have to put it down in order to free their hand and meet yours half way.

(3) Smile ☺

There is nothing like a warm beaming greeting that will soften someone up. A warm smile is the best weapon against indifference. Most people are defenseless when they are suddenly confronted with a friendly smile. Just look at the smiley face above, doesn't it give you at least a small sense of happiness? When I am confronted with a person and I see them smile at me, I feel obligated to smile back; it breaks the ice. A beautiful, sincere smile is a non-verbal gesture that conveys to others that you "come in peace!"

> *"As the sun warms the sand, so*
> *a smile warms the heart."*
> Emerson P. Davis

A simple smile and proper greeting can turn a Beast into a Beauty!

(4) Eye contact

Eye contact is a psychological must. If you cannot maintain eye contact, it may be perceived by others that you have something to hide. Whenever you approach someone, look at her straight into her eyes and have your eyes communicate to her that you are one confident, strong, sincere, and trustworthy individual. Without eye contact, you might as well say to the person to whom you are addressing: "Hi, I am a loser and I cannot be trusted. I have no confidence, my dog hates me and I am constipated! Have a good day."

Along with eye contact you should be aware of your handshake: A solid handshake can go a long way. (This is equally true for men as well as women.) A solid handshake tells people that you are strong, confident and you have a purpose. A weak, flimsy handshake conveys a message that you are insecure and are quite frail. If you don't believe me, try it on someone and watch his or her facial expressions. They will likely react squeamishly.

(5)   Enthusiasm sells!

I love to be around people with an abundance of energy; they just seem to light up the room upon entry. People that speak with enthusiasm are admired because it is a trait that relatively few have mastered. If you wish to sound enthusiastic, speak with optimism in your voice. Be optimistic and see the good things that are in your life. If you develop a habit of seeing your happiness every-single-day, you will project that happiness through your enthusiasm for life.

People who have learned to speak with enthusiasm have learned the secret rule of engagement. They have learned how to captivate people via, a unique, infectious energy. They have learned to see the good in others and focus on those characteristics. They don't have their heads buried in the sand. They know that there are good and bad people in the world; they simply choose to give people the benefit of the doubt. This is how they have developed a positive karma; it is their choice. They choose to be optimistic and project that optimism for themselves and others. These are people who even sound interesting ordering a pepperoni pizza; enthusiasm sells because people are attracted to this energy like a magnet attracts steel.

(6) Be Articulate

In America, the English language appears to be under a ferocious attack by its archenemy, "Slang!" Slang's weapon of choice: laziness and the unwillingness to care. Perhaps proper grammar is simply not accepted on the streets or within the high schools; but why is it slowly becoming accepted in the business arena? This is a territory where poor grammar does not belong. If poor grammar must exist, feel free to keep it where it belongs: on the streets where people are more open to disorder.

We must accept that in life, there are rules that must be preserved. There are rules in driving, games, stock trading, accounting, marriage, architecture, religion and so on and so forth. Even gravity has a rule that we rely on: "What goes up, must come down." In virtually every facet of our life there are rules and these rules are not only preserved, they are also protected. In regards to the rules of language, the same commitment must be maintained. The rules of language must be fostered and protected in schools, businesses and especially during your presentations. In essence, proper grammar should be used, respected and nurtured. Don't be afraid to continuously learn; mastering the art of language is a lifetime endeavor.

(7) Understanding

This important topic was covered extensively above; therefore I will not be repetitive. With that said, the topic of "understanding" is a topic worthy of a quick review. If you do not understand why, you need to consider our history and what has occurred and will continue to occur when there is a *lack* of understanding. In summary, the lack of understanding leads mankind to war, death, hatred, argument, intolerance, and revenge (to name a few areas of disparity).

Test yourself. When was the last time you thought: "I do not understand why somebody would act in such a manner?" To the point, just because you do not understand, does not make it wrong. It does make it beyond your scope of comprehension because your experiences would not lead you to the same conclusion. This is *understandable* because we all have different experiences that make us unique. This is important to consider whenever you are quick to judge someone else or when someone else is judging you.

With regard to conversations, think of each conversation as a journey and in order for the journey to be successful, all parties involved must venture down the same path. If you have an understanding of why the person is telling you something, or if you understand the feelings and emotions of the person to whom you are speaking, you will both experience the same journey (or conversation) and grow. You will meet common ground and be more productive.

(8) Sincerity

If you have ever been around a person whose preference is to embellish the truth, you know how a person can easily lose credibility with others. In my opinion, it is easy to spot this type of person; all they need to do is speak for a short amount of time and they will show his or her true colors.

Essentially, there is no substitute for an honest and sincere reputation. The person with whom you are in communication will want you to be sincere. Once people see you as an honest and sincere person, they will want to speak and work with you because they will trust you. On the contrary, once you are labeled as an individual who lacks sincerity, most people disengage themselves from you. Be true to others and you will be true to yourself. In a word, be *honest*.

If you are going to ask: "How are you doing?" Do so with sincerity in your voice and eyes. Don't ask in the same indifferent manner that most people do. In addition, ask how the family is doing; people usually love to discuss their children. The main point is, in order to be viewed as a sincere listener, you must not only listen with your ears, you must also listen with your eyes, your spirit, your heart, your mind, and your gestures. This is how you will get people to further trust you and open up to you. Whether it is a potential client, your child, spouse, boss, employee, a stranger, or a friend, sincerity in a conversation enables trust, thereby encouraging others to open, not only their mouths, but also their hearts. Hence, while you converse, be sincerely sincere.

(9) Modesty

> *For by the grace given me I say to every one of you: Do not think of yourself more highly than you ought, but rather think of yourself with sober judgment, in accordance with the measure of faith God has given you.*
> ROMANS 12:3

Modesty is a human attribute that is underrated by American society. The antonym of modesty should not be confused with confidence. The Antonym of modesty is flamboyance, vanity or conceit. Just because one acts in a confident manner does not mean one is flamboyant, pretentious or vain. In short, people who have a combination of modesty and confidence in their voice and mannerisms are respected and admired for those traits. A modest or humble person is non-threatening and easier to trust and communicate with than a person whose words and ego are full of pride. Be confident but modest while you are in communication with others. It was C.S. Lewis in his book *Mere Christianity*, who wrote:

"If you are in the habit of looking down on people, you will not have the time to look up to God."

(10) Credibility through Knowledge

If you plan on making statements, make sure you know what you are talking about. Be factual and be able to support those facts with credible resources. With that said, people will believe your statements if those statements are accurate, well thought out and articulated in a structured, concise, easy to follow and confident manner. Think back to the last time you spoke with a person regarding a topic for which you had a profound understanding. That was a time that you, more than likely, spoke with energy, passion, and confidence. Now think back to a time you tried to have a conversation about a topic for which you had little knowledge; you probably lacked the same spark that you had when you did have the necessary level of knowledge. If you know little about the topic you are discussing, it is more admirable to admit it, than to be misleading and deliver misinformation.

The more I know, the more I realize I know less of what I thought I knew!

To illustrate the importance of becoming as knowledgeable as you can before you attempt to articulate that knowledge, find one sipping straw and one toilet paper roll and take both items to any picture hanging on a wall. Be certain that it is a picture for which you have never seen nor have any prior knowledge. Next, (without looking at the picture) stand three feet away from the picture and place the sipping straw to one eye while keeping the other eye closed. Now, look through the tiny hole of the straw and look at one spot of the picture. You will see only a very small portion of the picture. You will, therefore, gain very limited knowledge of the picture. Sure, you see the picture, however, due to such limited vision (the diameter of the straw), you have learned little about the picture.

If I were to ask you to articulate what you know about the picture, you will not sound very knowledgeable if you make an attempt. If you do make an attempt to inform me about the scenery or, for that matter, any details about the picture, you will surely sound ignorant. This is especially true if I am aware of the subtleties of the picture. In essence, you basically have not seen nor learned enough about the picture, due to your limited vision and experience, to speak intelligently about the picture in question.

Next, pick up the toilet paper roll and look through the hole at the same spot of the picture. Your knowledge of the picture has just increased. You can see much more of the picture, therefore you are more likely to be able to have a better explanation regarding the picture. Your vision and knowledge about the picture are still limited, however, you have more knowledge than when you only looked through the straw hole because the diameter of the toilet paper roll is much wider.

Lastly, remove the toilet paper roll from your eye, look at the picture without anything restricting your vision and study the details of the picture. You are now ready to have an intelligent conversation about the picture. You are much more likely to be able to answer most questions I have about the scenery, colors, framing, characters and theme of the picture. You will sound much more knowledgeable and, thus, credible during the discussion. Consequently, I will be more inclined to trust you.

To the point, be knowledgeable about the topic by being prepared to discuss the topic. Have a full view of the picture before you plan on discussing it or before you plan on presenting it to an audience. Should your knowledge be limited (as if you had a narrow view) work diligently to expand your knowledge about that specific topic. Should you not know enough, be honest. If you attempt to discuss a topic or issue for which you have limited knowledge or experience, similar to having limited knowledge or experience due to your viewing a picture through the hole of a sipping straw, your confidence, rightfully so, will also be limited. Consequently, as mentioned above, so will your credibility. You will basically be perceived as a person who has tunnel vision. Be trustworthy and be concise, and you will be one step closer to acquiring the Power of Conversation as you REACH Presentation Skills and inspire others.

(11) Inquisitive

This is the perfect time to emphasize the importance of asking questions. If your knowledge is limited, ask questions. Ask open-ended questions that are relevant to the conversation and topic. Don't ask questions that will give you a simple yes or no response. Ask questions such that the response will enable you to drill down to the core of the topic or issue. If you are a good listener, you will find opportunities to discover more from the person with whom you are conversing, if you plunge deeper into the dialogue. This is especially important if your level of knowledge on the topic is limited. The best way to take such a plunge is to ask in-depth, open-ended questions. Three goals will be accomplished:

1. You will learn more from the person you are addressing.
2. You will demonstrate to the person who is speaking that you find his or her dialogue interesting.

3. You will be more prone to establish rapport or, better yet, an acquaintance or friendship simply because you are engaged.

(12) Be Objective

> *Pride only breeds quarrels, but wisdom is found in those who take advice.*
> Proverbs 13:10

As taught by eastern philosophers, it is meaningful to remain objective when you converse with others because often, personal growth is a result of learning from others. When you remain close-minded you see only your ideas, your thoughts and your experiences. To remain close-minded is to remain ignorant of many other possibilities, visions, and flavors. To quote Bruce Lee from his book *TAO OF JEET KUNE DO*, "Empty your cup so that it may be filled; become devoid to gain totality."[2] In essence, come to the table with an empty cup, so you can experience different drinks. Admittedly, this is no easy task because we spent years, or even decades, developing our personal views. If we practice being objective and we are at times successful in this endeavor, we may find that it pays off in dividends. Advocated by Henry Ford, the founder of Ford Motor Company, "Anyone who stops learning is old, whether at twenty or eighty. Anyone who keeps learning stays young. The greatest thing in life is to keep your mind young."

Another reason it is vital for all of us to be more objective as we journey through the days of our lives, is due to the growing diversity in our country. People from all around the world continue to migrate to America. In addition, technology enables people, from various continents, to cross over oceans and communicate with each other with a click-of-a-mouse. These are people with various backgrounds, cultures, religious beliefs and thought processes. For each of us to be successful, we must be more sensitive to these facts. This point is especially critical during business interactions. Therefore, if you are about to present or conduct business with a potential customer who is from a different country, it is important to familiarize yourself with his or her customs. This is especially true if you are going abroad to conduct business.

(13) Get to the Point!

This important topic was covered extensively above so I will not drive home this *point* any longer. Essentially, while you are conversing or presenting, make certain you remain focused on your objective. Be an archer and engage your target by staying focused on your point. Be flexible and allow for the twists and turns that are inevitable within the course of the conversation, but always remain aware of your point. Close the conversation with some type of action or commitment from the person you are attempting to influence. That certainly will be a key indicator of whether or not you achieved your objective and were able to remain steadfast on your point.

In summary, the aforementioned are simple tips and techniques that can assist anyone with improving on the Power of Conversation. Once you practice these techniques and get more comfortable with them, you will find that it will become automatic, a new habit. If you can converse with the right word(s), and all the other previously mentioned imperatives, you will earn someone's trust. Once you establish trust, the person with whom you are conversing will be more likely to open up to you.

There is an alternative. You can be one of those selfish, narrow-minded speakers; i.e., Mr. Joshua. The type that nobody wishes to listen to in the first place. Think about it, I am sure each one of us has experienced this scenario at least once in our life. Somebody just talks and talks, however, saying nothing at all. Do people fight to speak with you, or do you find others are fighting to keep their eyelids apart when you are speaking? Do you find others hanging onto every one of your words, or do they appear to be hanging from a cliff, with no place to go, but down? Are others anticipating your next sentence, or are they anticipating the perfect opportunity to subtly slip away? "Well, I have to go now." These are the questions you have to ask yourself while you are engaged in conversation. In order to answer those questions, you have to be sensitive to the actions and reactions of others.

Remember, in order for you to use the Power of Persuasion effectively and REACH Presentation Skills, you must first improve on the Power of Conversation. Make the conversation enjoyable to all participants. It is much like kissing; if you are only concerned with your pleasures, you will be the only one enjoying the kiss. REACH Presentation Skills by realizing that the Power of Conversation is not the gift to gab; it is an acquired skill that first comes from within each of us. Understanding this is the true gift.

"What lies behind us and what lies before us are small matters compared to what lies within us."

-Oliver Wendell Holmes
Famous Writer

SECTION TWO

2

SECTION TWO

The Power of Persuasion

The

Power

of

Persuasion

Your job is to tailor each discussion to fit each individual's needs, just as the job of a seamstress is to tailor a suit to fit each individual's needs; indeed, one size does not fit all!

The dolphin is the most beautiful marine mammal that God has ever created. *It has so many wondrous characteristics. For centuries, the marine dolphin has entertained sailors with their antics and apparent friendliness as they frolic alongside cruising ships. To be able to witness such a beautiful creature soar through the air and flip, effortlessly, is indeed a spectacular and unique experience. Imagine how elated, amazed and surprised the sailors must have felt when their eyes were bequeathed, for the very first time, with the sights of a marine dolphin and its remarkable display of aquatic feats. (A gift is always appreciated more when it is unexpected.) For these and other reasons, man has been intrigued with the marine dolphin for centuries.*

More recently however, the dolphin, more specifically the bottle-nosed dolphin or Tursiops Truncatus, has captivated researchers' attention for reasons that go beyond entertainment. To name one, most marine dolphins have a large repertoire of unique sounds. The two sounds that I will focus on include the pulsed sounds of two general types: Those emitted in emotional states and those used for echolocation (Sonar).

Burst-Pulse Sounds: <u>Emotional State</u>

Dolphins do not have vocal chords, so they obviously cannot communicate with the same capacity that humans can, however, they are still very capable of communicating effectively to other dolphins. If you have ever seen a dolphin perform at a marine show you, more than likely, have been exposed to its more obvious form of communication. This form is called the pure-tone sounds; you would identify these sounds as whistles and chirps. It is suggested that dolphins can determine not only which type of species and school another dolphin represents, but also its emotional state, simply by listening to these sounds. Furthermore, it is suggested that a dolphin can emit a variety of burst-pulse sounds and these sounds permit a dolphin to communicate their emotional state to other dolphins. Although these sounds are distinguishable to other dolphins, humans have not been able to differentiate one burst-pulse sound from another and, therefore, cannot identify the emotional state of a dolphin by these sounds. In short, these sounds are too similar to the human ear.

Burst-Pulse Sounds: _Echolocation/SONAR_

The power of the Atlantic Ocean adds to the dolphins' mystic. For centuries, man has been trying to conquer this powerful body of water. Once upon a time, man was fooled by his arrogance in believing that he was able to build an "infallible and unsinkable ship." The Atlantic Ocean must have been more than skeptical. Its skepticism soon turned into a chilling reality; a reality that is now marked indelibly in the history of man. It was as if the Atlantic Ocean demanded respect and, soon after, was awarded with that respect the night it made a statement that would echo across every continent around the world and into future generations. That everlasting statement was made the night the Atlantic swallowed up that "unsinkable" ship in a matter of hours. After that night of terror and for decades thereafter, everyone around the civilized world would be familiar with the name, Titanic.

A grand name was appropriately given to a spectacular ship. Such a grand name would prove to reflect man's arrogance when he made such unsinkable claims. The word, "titanic" is defined as "gigantic" in Merriam Webster's dictionary. Although man believed the Titanic was gigantic, the Atlantic Ocean must have seen it more as a mere skiff (a very small boat) and treated it as such. Now, the word Titanic is hauntingly recognized across the Atlantic Ocean and around the world. In fact, the Titanic is more than an eerie reminder of the ocean's mystical power; it is a name that continues to accentuate man's fallibility.

This powerful and enigmatic liquid underworld is what the dolphin calls home and, as mentioned earlier, this home is another element that adds to the dolphins' mystic. Within this vast ocean and among the many nameless sea-creatures, vegetation, lost ships and dark unknowns, is a frontier full of predators in murky waters. How is such a beautiful creature, like the dolphin, able to call this dark and ominous body of water, home?

One answer is found within a vibration and that vibration is called Echolocation. Echolocation is one means by which the dolphin can, not only communicate with other dolphins, but also learn the whereabouts of its surroundings, other dolphins, materials, and seamounts. A dolphin's unique capability of emitting echolocation (sounds or sonar) may go as *far as one half to one mile away. This keen ability of remote detection by transmitting a pulse allows a dolphin to familiarize itself with its environment even in the darkest depths of the ocean, where its eyes will fail. The dolphin generates clicking sounds and waits for those sounds to rebound off an object and come back to it. The dolphin can determine how close the object is by how long it takes for its sound to echo back to it.*

Whether it is for the technical way they can communicate, the way they frolic, or simply for your viewing pleasures, you can imagine the many fine qualities that add to the dolphins' beauty. Quite simply, the way they bring joy to researchers and laypersons alike should be considered invaluable.

To illustrate, the way a dolphin appears to smile always makes a human smile right back at it; it is contagious. The way a dolphin will care for its young will create a chill to run down a loving human parent's spine. The way a dolphin will fool around will bring joy to a child's face. The way a dolphin can leap from the sea to twenty feet up in the air, much like a missile, will impress even the best of gymnasts. The way a dolphin can "showoff" its inspiring physical strength will impress the world's strongest man. The sleek and sculptured physique of a dolphin will impress a body builder. The dolphin has even been found to temporarily alleviate human beings' physical pain, simply by swimming with them and this impresses medical doctors. In short, the bottle-nosed dolphin touches a broad spectrum of human lives and for this reason I am convinced that this wonderful creature is the most beautiful marine mammal God has ever created!

DO YOU AGREE?

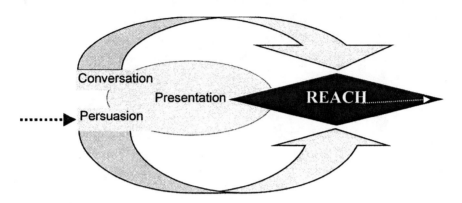

Conversation
Presentation
Persuasion
REACH

Are you persuaded?

You are probably wondering what dolphins have to do with the Power of Persuasion. I am demonstrating the importance of supporting a claim. If you make a claim or statement and your intent is to do it informatively and/or persuasively, you must thoroughly support that claim with intelligent and knowledgeable dialogue and/or facts. For example, in the beginning of the dolphin exposition, I made an explicit claim: "The Dolphin is the most beautiful marine mammal that God has ever created!"

Would you be persuaded and agree with this statement if I simply made this claim, however, without the supporting exposition? Which one of the following two has more impact?

⇒ Make a claim and then ask if one agrees with the claim

⇒ Make a claim, support the claim with intelligent, knowledgeable and informative facts, and then ask if one agrees with the claim

Obviously, the latter is more informative and persuasive because it "paints a picture" for the one being addressed. Painting a picture is the effect of my due diligence. I simply find facts by way of research, which enables me to, not only learn more about the dolphin, but also illustrate some of its interesting features in a more comprehensive and descriptive fashion. For example, I was able to learn the way in which the dolphin communicates, via, burst-pulse sounds and echolocation. I then express those facts in a well-designed, thought-out manner. My exposition, however, does not end with those technical facts. I also consider another approach. I compare a dolphin's attributes to a human's attributes; i.e., smiling, taking care of its young, alleviating pain, the way the dolphin frolics, and the dolphin's physical strength. I am illustrating those features with the intent to generate understanding through association. Finally, I am attempting to illustrate how the bottle-nosed dolphin affects a wide variety of people in so many different and wondrous ways. In short, I am giving you reasons why I believe the dolphin is the most beautiful marine mammal that God has ever created.

Now, shortly after I finish expressing these facts about the dolphin, a gentleman named William walks up to you and says the following:

"I couldn't help but over-hear your conversation about the dolphin. I completely disagree with Mr. Carbone. I believe the killer whale is the most spectacular mammal in the ocean. I don't know why, I just think they're really neat! Don't you agree that the killer whale is more spectacular?"

Are you going to be persuaded by such a statement? If you are objective, there is little probability that you would be persuaded. William never gave you a reason to be persuaded because he did not once support his claim with intelligent discourse, facts or illustrations. William fell short of a good persuasive discussion, he was not successful in painting a picture, he did not support his claim and he certainly did not establish any credibility with you. These are the elements that are necessary for a good, informative or persuasive discussion.

If you can paint a picture, demonstrate features and benefits, and illustrate facts that add weight and credibility to your claim or argument, you will be much more effective in the Power of Persuasion. If you disregard the importance of supporting your claim, you will very likely fail to meet your goal. For example, to be successful in the sale's arena, you must have, not only a good product with valuable features, you must also have good product knowledge, which will enable you to present your product's features intelligently. Without product knowledge, you will lose credibility with the person you are attempting to influence. Just think back to the last time you were listening to a person who was attempting to persuade someone, however, was ineffective with their effort. What did that person do wrong? He was more than likely using ill-informed, less than credible and narrow-minded logic as a tool to accomplish his goal. Or, he may have failed to give any reason at all to persuade another. Being prepared with accurate information is one of the most credible and useful ways to master the Power of Persuasion and REACH Presentation Skills.

Are you persuaded that the bottle-nosed dolphin is the most beautiful marine mammal that God has ever created? Some may agree while others may disagree. This is rational but I would hope that I, at the very least, enabled those of you who have not been persuaded, to contemplate the so many wonderful traits that make the dolphin unique and beautiful. Did you learn something? If you did, you are probably one step closer to being persuaded than if you had learned nothing at all. Additionally, if you believe the information that I provided to be informative and credible, you will likely take the time to listen to me in the future.

Query: What is one's objective when one attempts to persuade another?

If you immediately answer the following: "The goal is persuasion, to influence another to agree with your thoughts on an issue, product, ideology or topic." If this is your response, you are partially correct. (Only partially.) You must have more than one goal in mind while you are attempting to persuade or influence another.

To put it in perspective, consider the following scenario: Imagine a rectangular box that is ten-foot in height, six-foot in length, and five-foot in width that is built with transparent glass walls. Positioned inside and on the bottom of this glass box is a large fan with the switch set on maximum speed. In addition to a large fan, there is a relatively large quantity of one, five, and ten-dollar bills, which are getting blown all around a woman named Pam. What is Pam doing inside the glass box filled with airborne money? She is flailing and waving her arms almost uncontrollably as if she were getting attacked by a swarm of bees. Why is Pam flailing her arms so hysterically? She has an objective; to grab as much money as she possibly can within a twenty-second time frame. Tick-tock, tick-tock, and her twenty-second time limit is complete. The fan stops blowing; all the money that was flying in the air, loses its support and ceases to flutter above and around Pam. Each airborne bill gently, but acrobatically, flips, twists and turns its way down to the floor of the box. The glass door opens. The crowd begins to cheer as Pam walks out of the glass box with thirty-five dollars and a really bad hairdo. Not bad for twenty-seconds of work.

A few minutes later, a woman named Alice is chosen to enter the glass box filled with money. The fan, once again, gets turned on to maximum speed and the money, subsequently, becomes airborne. She looks out at the crowd, who is looking back at her, and she proceeds to smile as she ignores the money that is flying all around her. Seconds later, she casually bends all the way down to the floor of the box and gathers all the money that never got off the ground. She then proceeds to deliberately pluck the larger bills off the motionless pile of money. Within ten seconds, she has as much money as she could possibly place in her hands and she proceeds to walk out of the box; in addition to the cash, she is leaving the box with a big smile and a really bad hairdo.

In retrospect, Alice had approximately five-seconds remaining on the clock, however, she felt as if she had completed her mission because her hands were full of money and she could not reach and grasp any more. She walked out of the glass box with approximately five hundred dollars. The crowd was hysterical. That is not bad for twenty-seconds of work! Why was Alice four hundred and sixty five dollars more successful than Pam?

The answer is simple. If you want to be successful, you must remain focused on your task, goal or objective and you must do so with a plan of action. If you are placed in a glass box and your goal is to accumulate as much money as you can possibly take hold of and you have twenty seconds to succeed, remain focused on the largest pile of money and the largest increments of dollar bills. The same type of focus is also important when it comes to the Power of Persuasion. If you want to persuade someone of something, you must remain focused on your task, goal or objective and you must do so with a plan of action. Within that plan, you should include many, or all, of the imperatives listed in the pages that follow.

In the analogy, the first woman, Pam, did not maintain her poise. She knew that she had a chance to grab as much money as she could and she had to accomplish her goal within a twenty-second time limit. Thus, she started reacting and grabbing at whatever bill came within arm's reach. She did fair and she was rewarded with a fair sum of money for her time in the box. The second woman, Alice, however, did extremely well. She calmly acted with a plan of action. She understood that once she got into the glass box, she only had twenty-seconds to capture as much money as she could physically handle. She also knew that arbitrarily grapping into the air at whatever bill she could get her fingers around was not the most efficient means to accomplishing success with this venture. She understood that improvisation would cause her to fall short of her potential. Her plan of action was organized, well thought out and prepared. She was proactive and executed her plan with composure. Her success would follow because she worked effectively toward her goal.

The same principle is relevant with the Power of Persuasion as you REACH Presentation Skills. If you want to persuade or influence someone of something, you must be aware of your goal(s) and execute your plan of action. You must also be cognizant that you have more than one goal in mind. You must stretch beyond the obvious and consider the more important elements to the Power of Persuasion. You must be informative and be able to support your claims. In addition, as you continue your reading in this chapter, consider the elements of the previous chapter, the Power of Conversation. Both topics are interlinked. If you lack conversation skills, you cannot effectively employ the tactics of the Power of Persuasion and you will certainly not REACH Presentation Skills nor will you be inspirational.

Should this be a topic for which you are interested in researching further, I recommend reading, Zig Ziglar's *Secrets of Closing The Sale*. Many professional salespersons have more than likely read this book because he does a great job illustrating the technical components to salesmanship, persuasion, and "closing for action." With that said, what follows are techniques, which should help you learn the important components to the Power of Persuasion. If you are devoted to the following, you will more than likely learn to be an effective, persuasive speaker or valuable conversationalist. In addition, allowing yourself to develop and improve in these important skill sets will help you REACH Presentation Skills. Communication is a vehicle, which will help you get in the position to help yourself as well as others. Unless you have the wonderful ability to generate burst-pulse sounds to communicate and interpret, as dolphins do, you will most certainly benefit from the following techniques that I call, Lucky 13.

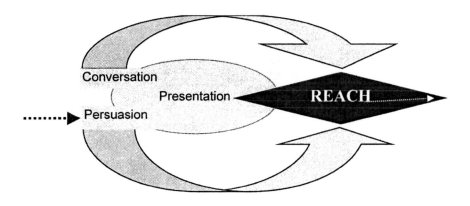

The Power of Persuasion

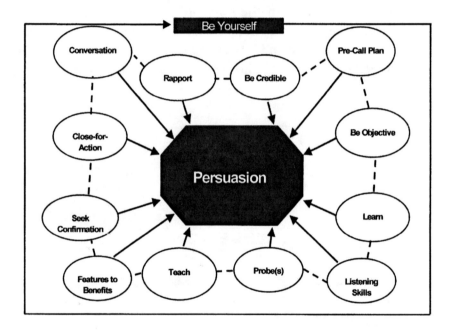

Imperatives for Mastering The Power of Persuasion
Lucky 13

(1) Persuasion

The first imperative is to remain aware of your primary goal, persuasion. How could you persuade someone of something if you do not have a goal? Like a hockey player, he has to know where to shoot the puck in order to score a goal. If not, someone will be there to block his shot with the intent of curbing his success. My primary goal was to convince you that *"The dolphin is the most beautiful marine mammal God has ever created!"* What means did I use to work toward my goal?

But first, what is persuasion? As I suggested above, persuasion is giving someone cause to understand the value of something as you understand the value of it. To persuade someone of something means you are influencing someone or converting someone from one frame of mind to another. To truly convert another person's way of thinking is no easy task. For this reason, there is more than one component to the Power of Persuasion. If you wish to be consistently successful, you must learn and execute the Lucky 13 imperatives to the Power of Persuasion.

(2) The Power of Conversation

Remember the many components of the previous chapter, the Power of Conversation, and be sure to utilize those skills accordingly when you are in front of the person you are attempting to influence. These skills are necessary because they intertwine with the Power of Persuasion. (Keep this important fact in mind while you are reading the remaining pages of this chapter.) If the conversation is mutually enjoyable and you are perceived to be articulate, credible and knowledgeable, you have likely established a rapport and that will get you one step closer to your goal.

(3) Rapport

> *"Do not let any unwholesome talk come out of your mouth, but only what is helpful for building others up according to their needs, that it may benefit those who listen."*
>
> EPHESIANS 4:29

Work on establishing rapport, not only *before* you begin attempting to persuade, but also during and after the persuasive *discussion*. I underscore the word persuasive *discussion* and not persuasive *argument* (as many would phrase it) because if you are attempting to influence someone, your discussion should not be considered, nor culminate to, an argument. The word discussion has a softer, friendlier connotation to it. Decades ago, when the use of old English was more prevalent than it is today, the word *argue* was a more positive word that had to do with reasoning or debating. That is no longer the case in America. Today, the word argument has a provoking undertone. For example, what follows are the American Heritage Dictionary's synonyms for the word argument: bicker, dispute, haggle, quarrel, squabble and wrangle. These are words that might cause you to start flailing in the air as if you are getting attacked by a swarm of bees while you are inside a glass box; or you may incite someone else to direct that state of madness towards you. When people begin to argue, they typically get emotional and personal and little good gets accomplished. This result is not going to be productive nor will you be in a position to establish a rapport with the person to whom you are speaking.

For example, in the short story that introduced section one of The Power of Conversation, Mr. Joshua had poor conversation skills. He was impatient, shortsighted and willingly prepared to aggressively argue his point to anyone. He ultimately illustrated his ineptness to Mercury. As a result, Mercury interpreted Mr. Joshua's visit as a disturbance. This irritated Mercury. As forewarned, he subsequently turned Mr. Joshua into an insect. Think about what some insects do to humans. They annoy us in many ways. One, in particular, is that they have the ability to transfer their venom to us, which we casually call a "sting." That sting and venom creates our skin to become irritated and it begins to itch. What do we do next? We do what we are not suppose to do, we scratch; thus, the beginning of a vicious itch-scratch cycle. The more you itch, the more you scratch. The more you scratch, the worse it gets because if the skin opens up from the scratching, you have the potential for a bacterial infection; in short, it worsens. The same can be said when two people get in an emotional argument. One person irritates another, then that person responds more aggressively, it escalates and the cycle continues; in short, it worsens.

To argue, as the word is defined today, is never a goal of mine when I am attempting to persuade someone of something. It is unlikely that one would establish rapport during an emotional argument. The next time you are attempting to persuade someone of something, put yourself in a glass box that is full of money and full of opportunity and not swarming bees. Conduct yourself as Alice successfully conducted herself. Her plan of action was organized, well thought out and prepared. She then executed her plan with composure. Her success would follow because she worked effectively toward her goal. She strategically put herself into a position that allowed her to pick the dollar bills that gave her the best value. The alternative is to react as if you are inside a glass box and you are getting attacked by a swarm of bees. The problem with the latter choice is that it could really sting in the end. (Ouch!) Pain is not the purpose of persuasion; persuasion is the purpose. Don't hurt yourself or others when you are attempting to help them understand your point-of-view or the value of your product or idea. Choose your words wisely and deliver them masterfully and you will be able to establish a rapport that will enable you to accomplish so much more, than if you had no rapport at all.

(4) Be Credible

> *"Whoever can be trusted with very little can also be trusted with much, and whoever is dishonest with very little will also be dishonest with much. So if you have not been trustworthy in handling worldly wealth, who will trust you with true riches?"*
>
> LUKE 16:10-11

To intentionally create and impart misinformation, or an embellishment of the truth, is synonymous to a used car salesperson who is in the habit of selling very old and corroded cars that have recently been covered with fresh coats of paint; eventually, the paint will peal, crack off and reveal the truth. One goal you should strive toward is to become known as an honest person; one who will offer credible and reliable information. Generally speaking, once credibility is lost, it is forever lost. It may be easier to find the famous staff of Moses before you can find your lost credibility. Moreover, it is just as important to *preserve* your credibility, as it is to *earn* your credibility. If you earn credibility, you earn trust; cherish its value and you will become more valuable.

Be perceived as an intelligent and concise speaker. The reason for being perceived as an intelligent speaker is obvious; the reasons for being perceived as a concise speaker may not be as obvious. You must get to the point and not "beat around the bush." Do not speak in a roundabout manner. For one reason, time is precious so you must respect the addressee's time. Read their mannerisms and determine whether or not they are waiting for the right moment to interrupt you and walk away. Secondly, you risk losing somebody's attention simply because you bored her with babbling dialogue. This is especially true during a presentation. You must read your audience by looking at their eyes. Their eyes will tell you if they are a fascinated audience or if you need to change the pace of your presentation.

Choose your words carefully and make your point. If your husband asks, "What time is it?" Don't build him a clock, just tell him the time. If your wife has a headache and asks you for two aspirins, don't add to her headache by informing her of the mechanism-of-action and the chemical structure of the aspirin; just hand her two tablets and one glass of water. If your son wants to learn how to drive a car, don't hand him the blueprints to building a car; teach him the mechanics of driving a car. If your customer wants to know what the features are to a computer, do not give her information that would exceed the memory of that computer. In essence, be selective with your vocabulary and refrain from being verbose and/or redundant. Get to the point!

Choosing the fewest words possible should always be your goal. (Unless you are creating a filibuster.) The best way to learn how to choose the fewest words is by obtaining good in-depth knowledge of the topic you are about to discuss. In simplest terms, be prepared. If you are searching for words to make the dialogue make sense, it will be obviously disorganized and you risk losing credibility. Carefully choose your dialogue and be intelligent, confident and concise. In short, be prepared by researching and studying the topic and then practice your delivery before you present it. If you don't find it easy to articulate your idea or presentation, then you haven't practiced enough. Being concise, prepared and knowledgeable will add to, and not take away from, your credibility. Be prepared by preparing a pre-call plan.

(5) Pre-call Planning (Plan of Action)

As mentioned above, you must be prepared if you want to be perceived by others as a credible resource; thus, it is important to have a pre-call plan or plan of action. How often have you finished a conversation with someone else and, as you are walking away, you think of something intelligent you should have said that could have helped drive your point? You find yourself saying, "Darn-it, I should have said..." If you put more energy into a pre-call plan, or a plan of action, before you begin your discussion or presentation, you will be more likely to have intelligent dialogue during the discussion or presentation. Take advantage of the opportunity you are given by being perceived as a credible speaker. As mentioned above, a pre-call plan adds to your credibility.

In addition, a pre-call plan will accomplish other deeds: it will help you be more concise, help you develop your direction, keep you focused on your goal, aid you with being more informative, and help you be prepared for possible hidden or stated objections. A good pre-call plan will also help you persuade someone because it will teach you more about the individual you are addressing. You will also, very likely, learn what is important to the addressee. You may even come to understand some of that person's actions. Once you learn what is important to that person or understand that person's actions, you are able to focus on those specifics, intelligently, concisely and confidently.

For example, I may learn by my pre-call plan that you take a very humanistic and sensitive approach to situations within your business. You see the *value* of human being's nurturing ways and manifest this humanistic approach by your decisions and actions. Once I determine these important facts, I decide to put into my pre-call plan, the various ways I can compare a dolphin's actions to a human being's actions.

⇒ "The way a dolphin will care for its young will always create a chill to run down a loving parent's spine."

⇒ "The way a dolphin appears to smile always makes a human smile right back at it; a dolphin's smile is contagious!"

⇒ "The dolphin has even been found to temporarily alleviate human being's physical pain, simply by swimming with them, and this impresses medical doctors."

If I did not learn something valuable about you, come to understand you or if I did not take the time to learn what you may find most important, i.e., sensitivity, human emotions and the willingness to nurture, I may have taken a more technical approach while I was attempting to persuade you. As a result of this approach, I may be less likely to retain your attention. How can I persuade you if you find no interest in what I have to say? In short, if you put forth the effort to do a plan of action, you should be more prepared to handle most any situation that may confront you. The pre-call plan or, plan of action, is a valuable tool that is worth the extra effort, particularly when you REACH Presentation Skills with the intent of inspiring others.

There are a variety of tactics or tools that you can inculcate into your personal or business life, which will assist you to become better prepared prior to an important conversation or presentation. The best tactics or tools you can implement are those you develop yourself. The reason for that is due to the fact that you know your history, product and ideas better than the one who may be consulting you. You understand the people in your life and the behaviors you wish to alter. You are aware of your prospects and customers and what drives them. Therefore, you can best customize your own algorithm or pre-call plan. You will be amazed at just how much you learn as you proceed to think about and build your own, customized rendition.

With that said, see below for an example of a basic pre-call plan that you can either, use for yourself, or use as a guide as you build and customize your own. What is important is that you put a lot of thought into your important discussion because that discussion is an opportunity for you to be great and inspire. The funny thing about the results of those opportunities is that those results come in a variety of flavors: some quite tasty, while others are downright distasteful. Quite often, the final result is due to the ingredients that you put, or fail to put, into your mix.

Anatomy of a Pre-Call Plan

With whom I am going to speak and what is the purpose?

What general relevant history do I know about this individual? Have I met this individual in the past? If yes, what should I expect?

What is the idea, product, or behavior and why do I want to influence this person with my idea, product or behavior?

What will this individual consider important?

What are three top objections I can anticipate?

    1.

    2.

    3.

How should I be prepared to handle each objection?

    1.

    2.

    3.

What will success look like after this conversation or presentation?

Verbalize the following to yourself:
"Because I completed this plan, I am now ready to be inspirational!"

(6) Be Objective During the Dialogue or Exposition

As previously illustrated, you can learn from the person, to whom you are speaking, if you do a pre-call plan; however, the learning should not stop there. During your dialogue, you must also try to learn more about that person and what he or she knows about the topic being discussed. This should occur during your discussion. Be objective and attempt to see situations and experiences through his or her eyes. This will permit you to accomplish many goals. To name a few, you will learn what is important to the person you are addressing, learn something about the said topic, develop a two-way communication and make the conversation more enjoyable to all parties involved. As a result, you will establish a rapport. You will also learn how to be more concise. You may even come to understand that person and, as thoroughly covered in the previous chapter, that understanding could make a critical difference. So, what is the advantage to being unprejudiced? You may learn something of value.

(7) Learn

Above, in the segment sub-titled "Be Objective," I referenced the importance of learning from the prospect or the person you are addressing. More specifically, I referenced the importance of learning what the prospect believes to be important within your product, presentation or dialogue. Yes, it is important for you to teach the prospect the value of something, as you understand its value; however, doesn't it stand to reason for you to learn from the prospect what are his or her "hot-buttons?" It is critical for you to learn what is important to the person you are attempting to persuade. Once you gain that salient information, then you can focus on that particular area of interest.

For example, I may have learned that the person I am addressing is a former Naval Officer:

"Sir, I understand you were once in the navy and you worked on a submarine. Aren't you amazed with the similarities between that vessel's sonar system and the dolphins' innate ability to emanate echolocation vibrations?"

Chances are, that question will open a two-way dialogue and, therefore, lead to many possibilities. To name one, I am going to learn from him what he understands about echolocation and even if he sees the value of it. If he is well versed on this topic, I am going to consider this moment as an opportunity and learn as much as I can about echolocation. Moreover, I am going to learn if this topic peaks his interest and, therefore, one worth focusing our attention. This could be the one element that persuades him that the *dolphin is the most beautiful marine mammal that God has ever created.*

The point is, there may be a variety of features to your product or idea; however, it may be necessary to discuss only a few of those features. Ask yourself the following:

> ⇒   Do I need to illustrate every feature possible to make my point?
> ⇒   Would it be advantageous to focus most of our attention and time on the few areas the person, to whom I am speaking, believes to be most important and interesting?

The only way to do the latter is to learn (and not guess) what he believes to be important about the topic. How is this task accomplished? By mastering all the components of the Power of Conversation and the Power of Persuasion.

The above former navy officer example, as it compares to the humanitarian example, demonstrates the importance of highlighting different features for different people. Each person has his or her unique personality, interests, thoughts, experiences and understandings. Your job is to tailor each conversation or presentation to fit each individual's needs, just as the job of a seamstress is to tailor a suit to fit each individual need. One size does not fit all when it comes to suits, prospects, customers, children, colleagues or friends.

When I take into consideration the former navy officer's experiences, I'm going to focus most of our attention on the innate technology of the dolphin and how it compares to a submarine's sonar capabilities; I will then respond accordingly. In sharp comparison, remember the humanitarian example I used in the section entitled pre-call plan? He may be influenced specifically by the way I highlight the similar traits that humans and dolphins appear to share. I certainly did not believe it was as important to focus his attention on the technical discussion I had with the former navy officer. Essentially, I must learn from the person, to whom I am speaking, what he or she finds most stimulating and try to avoid discussing the features he or she finds least stimulating.

How should I attempt to persuade another that the dolphin is the most beautiful marine mammal that God has ever created? It depends on with whom I'm speaking, what I have learned during my pre-call plan, and what I will continue to learn throughout my discussion. It depends on what I have learned, not only about that person, but also what I have learned from that person. So, what is one invaluable skill you must employ to accomplish these lofty goals? You must use your God given gift to listen.

(8) Listening Skills

> *A wise man will hear and increase learning,*
> *and a man of understanding will attain wise*
> *counsel, to understand a proverb and an enigma,*
> *the words of the wise and their riddles.*
> Proverbs 1:5-6

I wrote about the importance of effective listening skills in the Power of Communication, however, this skill cannot be stressed enough and is certainly appropriate for this chapter. After all, you cannot have efficient persuasive skills if you do not have efficient listening skills. With that said, I will not spend as much time on listening skills as I did in the previous section because the thoughts written in the previous section simply apply in this section. I will, however, give you two very short but interesting real life anecdotes, which are certainly applicable. The first anecdote translates how one's listening skills are effective, professional and courteous. The second anecdote is an extreme example of one's poor listening skills. It illustrates how this woman's deficiency in this critical area could make all parties involved look and feel downright foolish.

I was witness to the first short anecdote. It occurred in a small town in Georgia, which breeds the following set of questions: Is it true what they say about southern hospitality? Is it the culture of these smaller towns to be friendlier, kinder and more polite? If it is a culture, the actions related to southern hospitality are being taught by the adults and learned by their children. These lessons are being handed down from one generation to the next. In other words, they see the importance of being courteous to strangers, especially in a service oriented work environment. As for my opinion on the matter, I agree that this southern hospitality behavior is built into their culture because it is a behavior that has been and continues to be routinely practiced. This is a culture that we should all replicate, experience, and acknowledge as a valuable resource. Once acknowledged, we should import that valuable resource into all of our busy lifestyles.

The second anecdote happened to a colleague named Ron many years ago when he was a young, ambitious man seeking a career. It was during a job interview. By the end of the story, you will find it difficult to believe that it is based on a true story. It does illustrate the indifference that is outside of our homes. Whether it is this example or the many other poor experiences that unfortunately invade our lives upon many interactions, you have to wonder why. Why don't people care as much? Why have people become so unsympathetic? Why is there such apathy (a more descriptive word might be "droopiness!") with the employees who work in service oriented firms? Inspire yourself and others to truly listen and learn for as it is written in Proverbs 1:5, "a wise man will hear and increase learning and a man of understanding will attain wise counsel."

Anecdote number one: "The Waitress Gets It"

One day, I learned I could be impressed by a nineteen-year-old, part-time waitress' level of professionalism. To her, it was probably a simple and almost trivial act, however, to me (the customer) it was a very impressive demonstration of professionalism, customer service and good old-fashion southern hospitality.

It was moments after I gave her my dinner order. She noticed I was on a business trip and she took the time to establish a rapport with me. I am confident she really didn't care where I resided, but she was kind enough to engage in light conversation, if only for a minute or so. This is specifically the reason I was so impressed with her professionalism; I really wasn't talking about anything of great interest. Regardless, as I was in the middle of answering her question, I happen to notice that she was intently listening to me speak. Essentially, she had the type of eye contact that was telling me she was most intrigued with what I had to say. (Even if she may not have been at the least bit interested, her eyes and mannerisms were politely telling me she was listening.) In addition to her generous eye contact, she was diplomatic and skilled such that she asked relevant questions; again indicating to me that she was, in fact, paying special attention to the details of the conversation.

With that said, within a couple of minutes of our conversation, I noticed a young man (soon after I learned he was her friend) walking from one end of the restaurant headed toward a chair at the bar, which is located at the opposite end of the restaurant. The waitress and I could be found midway to his destination. As he approached this halfway point, I noticed him gently tap the waitress on the right shoulder as he walked by us and towards his seat at the bar. It was one of those scenarios where he was simply announcing his presence to her; acknowledging her, if you will, no more and no less. It was nonchalant and very brief, but I noticed it nonetheless.

I pretended not to notice the faint tap because I was in mid-sentence, however, I was anticipating a brief interruption from her. At the very least, I was expecting her eyes to leave mine, at least for an instant, while she greeted her friend shortly after the shoulder tap. It was at that moment I realized she was not going to miss one word I had to say. She made me feel as if those syllables coming out of my mouth were going to be the last sounds her ears would ever hear; the very last sounds. It was as if I was giving her stock tips and she was guaranteed to make money if she listened to my advice. In reality, we were basically exchanging in polite conversation and she was making me feel welcome at the restaurant.

Although I did not show it, I was astonished. Here is this bright nineteen-year-old girl, working a part-time-job, barely out of high school, not only *realizing* the good manners and overall relevance to having good listening skills for her customer, she was respectful enough and caring enough to actually follow through with it. Not only did she have the ability to do it, as most of us do, she also had the willingness to perform this skill at a high level. In short, I was so impressed with her realizing the importance of listening skills as an element of communication and business that I had to write about the experience in this book. If she is this service oriented, respectful and professional during small talk, imagine the level of professionalism she must have when she really has to depend on her listening skills in more serious situations.

As this nineteen-year-old, part-time waitress understood, there can be no substitute for good listening skills and overall professionalism. What the listener may perceive as a small, inconsequential disruption, the speaker may perceive as a lack of interest on the listener's part. Inevitably, the listener will lose the speaker's attention. If the listener discards the speaker's comments, the speaker may discard the listener because he may perceive the listener's non-verbal gesture as the following: "Your comments are not important enough for me to remain completely engaged."

Non-verbal gestures can be more powerful than words. What would the waitress be telling me had she looked away and started talking to her friend while I was in mid-sentence? Unfortunately, I know, as most of us do, because it happens all the time. This is especially true now that most of us own a cell phone. In school, we are taught that while we are speaking, we must consider and implement proper grammar. Unfortunately, there is not as much emphasis placed on the importance of listening. Most people either just don't get it, or really don't care.

Anecdote Number Two: "Time to Wake Up"

While we are on the subject of people not getting it or not caring enough to listen, it is now time to bring to light the second real life, humorous anecdote told to me by Ron. Some years ago, Ron was called in for a job interview by Company "X" and experienced a job interview he would not soon forget. When Ron, the interviewee, sat down and introduced himself to Mrs. "Doe," the interviewer, he was told that she did not have a chance to read his resume. His immediate thought was that she was not prepared and not interested enough in learning about potential employees. His first impression of her was that she lacked professionalism and interest.

He figured he should not be too hasty to judge and he should give her another chance. She then asked him to summarize his resume. Moments later, as he was sharing his credentials, he noticed that she was not engaged. She was looking around, fumbling through her papers and sorting her work, but he continued nonetheless. He persisted, that is, until her phone rang. She asked him to hold his thought as she proceeded to answer the phone. Ron's feelings were that it didn't matter who was on the phone; the interruption was inappropriate. After a few minutes of her rambling to the one on the other end of the phone, she hung up, looked at Ron and said, "Continue."

Ron decided that he should take a deep breath, get refocused and continue where he left off, and so he did. A couple of minutes later, as he was explaining his previous job experience, he became even more baffled. "Is it true, is this actually happening?" he asked himself, "Yes, I believe it is, she has fallen fast asleep."

She didn't slowly nod-off; she just closed her eyes, tipped her head toward her right shoulder, opened her mouth and fell fast asleep. Confounded, Ron stopped speaking while he was in the middle of a sentence and just gazed at her. What else could he do? He was amazed at her lack of professionalism. This untimely nap lasted for approximately five minutes.

Suddenly, as if an alarm went off in her head, she abruptly awoke, sat upright in her chair, looked at him straight in the eyes and said with excitement, "Your answer is exactly what I was looking for!"

Consequently, he decided to end the interview and seek alternative opportunities.

The situation that Ron experienced is unique, but it is a good illustration of how one's poor listening skills can make one look or feel outlandish. This is the reason it is important to allow the person speaking to finish his or her thoughts. It is important for the listener to be concerned and try to take interest in those thoughts so he or she can better understand the message the speaker is trying to convey. This is especially true when you are attempting to have an influence on another. So, how do you listen to and learn from the person you are attempting to influence? That is a good question! Speaking of questions…

(9) Probes

> *"A few decades ago, salespeople were taught that they should talk fast and dominate the conversation for fear that the prospect might ask a question they couldn't answer. We now understand we must probe not as a prosecuting attorney, but as a concerned individual who wants to become an assisting buyer."*[3]
>
> Renowned sales coach Zig Ziglar.

Merriam Webster's Pocket Dictionary defines the word "probe" as a slender instrument for examining a cavity. Furthermore, it defines a probe as an investigation; or to examine with a probe or to investigate. With regards to probes, NASA is certainly an institution that has learned the value of an effective probe (or set of probes). In fact, they have literally taken the probe to unprecedented heights. Two such probes, named the *Mars rover Spirit* and the *Mars rover Opportunity* have successfully flown 303 million-miles through space and landed on Mars, also known as, the Red Planet. The purpose of the Mars rover Spirit and the Mars rover Opportunity probes are to land on Mars gather information about Mars and send that information back to Earth. The aim of these probes is to investigate and learn about Mars. For example, to address the following question: Is there, or has there ever been, liquid water on Mars? If so, this finding may indicate the potential for life on Mars.

Do you believe it was important for NASA to send an estimated $820 million twin probe to Mars to learn more about Mars? In addition, do you believe executing the appropriate probes are, not only necessary, but also the most efficient means when attempting to gather specific information about Mars? The answer to both questions is absolutely. The appropriate probes are also essential when one is trying to learn more about the person one would like to influence. The point is, the appropriate set of probes, or set of questions, is dependent upon the situation as well as the person you are attempting to influence. You have to put some thought into your probes and customize them for the one with whom you are in conversation, just as NASA had to customize the Mars probes to get to, land on, and explore Mars. The right set of probes (questions) has the potential to be invaluable because it can lead you to unexplored paths and historical results.

The Journey To Mars

To illustrate, imagine yourself taking a passenger on a journey to Mars. You know basically where you both want to go, so you naturally begin flying up into the sky. You begin flying the passenger and yourself into space, mindlessly, but onward into space because you know Mars is somewhere up there. You also realize you have a vague map to Mars in your possession, however, the man you are flying is aware of the most direct route to Mars. He knows the quickest route to get from where you are now, liftoff from Earth, to your final destination, Mars.

Query: Do you, A, continue on your journey into outer space as the captain, the man with the rocket ship, the man with the vague map and, therefore, the man with all the control? Or, do you, B, risk losing some control and ask (probe for more information) the man sitting in the passenger seat of your rocket ship, which is the most direct route he would recommend taking?

Answer: Hopefully, you would answer the latter, B. Obviously learning from the passenger, who knows the shortest and most direct path to Mars, will save a lot of time and a lot of energy. Saving time and energy is typically the most desired route. So, why don't we always choose this course of action when we're attempting to influence someone of something?

Journey A =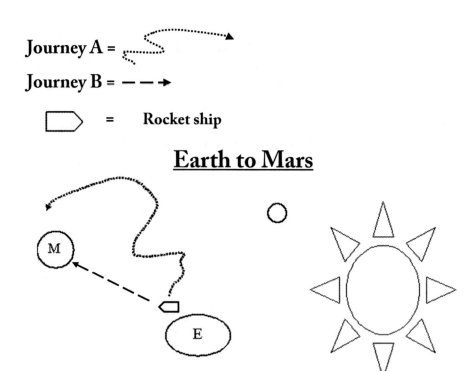

Journey B = – – →

⬡ **=** **Rocket ship**

<u>Earth to Mars</u>

The Journey To Your Destination

To illustrate: Imagine yourself taking a passenger (*the prospect/ addressee*) on a journey (*your sales presentation or a conversation on your idea*) to Mars (*your goal and purpose of the conversation*).

You know basically where you want to go
⇒ *Influence the addressee*

So you naturally begin flying into outer space
⇒ *Presenting your product, idea and/or materials*

You begin flying yourself and the passenger into orbit, mindlessly
⇒ *Just regurgitating as much information as possible with the hopes of persuading the addressee with something you say*

But onward you fly because you know it is what you are suppose to do as the captain of your rocket ship
⇒ *Talk and sell with the hopes you get no objections or questions*

Meanwhile, you are exhausting precious resources; i.e., time and fuel
⇒ *Talk and sell, talk and sell, time and patience is running out*

You also realize that you have a vague map to Mars in your possession
⇒ *Your presentation materials, illustrations or set of ideas*

However, the man you are flying to Mars knows the shortcuts and most direct route
⇒ *The specific information that is important/relevant to him. Keep in mind, it may be his view that there are only be a few "hot points." He may find only a few features important and it is your job to learn which ones*

In short, he knows the quickest route to get from where you are now, which is liftoff from Earth
⇒ *The beginning of the conversation or presentation*

To your final destination; in this case, Mars
⇒ *Persuasion, influencing a behavior, or the sale of your product or idea*

Let's examine this set of questions again: Do you, A, continue on your journey to Mars as the captain, the man with the rocket ship, the man with the vague map and, therefore, the man with all the control (*the man with all the information or sales material*)? Or, do you, B, risk losing some control and ask the passenger (*the prospect or addressee*), which is the quickest route he would recommend taking (*learning his needs, as well as, learning what materials and features he finds most interesting and relevant, as well as least interesting and least relevant*)?

Answer: Hopefully, you answered the latter, B. Obviously learning which path is the most direct path will save precious resources. This is typically the most desired route.

The Shortest Path From Earth to Mars

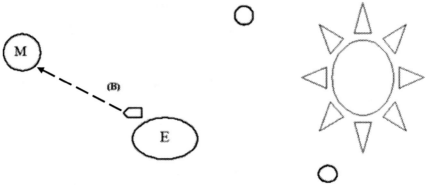

Always probe with the intent of learning from the person(s) you are attempting to persuade or influence. Not only do you want to teach the value of something, as you understand its value, you need to learn what is relevant and important to the prospect or addressee, as they understand its value. You must seek clarification and attempt to understand his or her reasoning. This will save all parties involved in the discussion or presentation, precious resources.

For example, I must learn from the former navy officer if he believes a dolphin's technical abilities are important and interesting. Or, I must learn from the humanitarian whether he perceives some of the humanistic traits that the dolphin demonstrates, to be fascinating.

These probes will help me better understand those individuals, tailor my presentation, help me get to the relevant points, and, ultimately, get me closer to persuading or influencing them.

Ask yourself the following: What is the effect of your message? How is the recipient receiving and interpreting your message? Take a lesson from NASA; the only way to learn, is to use a valuable set of probes. Fortunately, your probes will not cost you nearly as much as it cost NASA; nonetheless, that does not make your probes any less valuable to you.

(10) Teach

One of the two most under-rated and yet important elements to the Power of Persuasion is the importance of clarification and being informative. Did you teach the one you are attempting to influence anything of value? It is less likely that one will be persuaded if one does not understand the value of the topic or item as you understand its value. If you are trying to persuade someone of something in an effective manner, you must believe in it (or you will probably not be convincing) and in order for you to believe in it, you must understand the value of it. This is the reason pre-call planning or a plan-of-action is critical to success. With that in mind, you must ask yourself the following question before, during, and after your dialogue, exposition or presentation: "Did I teach those of whom I am in communication the value of this topic, product, or idea, as I understand its value?"

If you did, you are one step closer to persuasion. If you did not, how can he or she be persuaded? Chances are, he or she is not. To quote Zig Ziglar from his book, *Secrets of Closing the Sale:*

> *"When is it too early to close a sale? Too early is when you attempt to close before you have established in the prospect's mind significant value for what you are selling."4*

In order to demonstrate value, you must teach the person(s) you are addressing what the value is as you understand its value. For example, even if I did not persuade you that the dolphin is the most beautiful marine mammal God has ever created, one goal of my exposition was to teach you the value of the dolphin, as I appreciate the dolphins' value. I, at the very least, worked diligently to accomplish this goal. An example of my due diligence can be found in the way that I converted each feature of the dolphin into a potential benefit, which brings us to the next imperative.

Some benefits to teaching the addressee during the discussion/presentation:

> ⇒ Add value to the conversation
> ⇒ Adds to your credibility
> ⇒ Adds to your company's or family's credibility
> ⇒ You are more likely to develop a rapport with the addressee or audience
> ⇒ The addressee learns the value of your idea or product
> ⇒ You learn because anytime you teach something, you have to be prepared by learning the material or information in an advanced level
> ⇒ You are not wasting valuable resources; i.e., time, products
> ⇒ You are in a better position to "close-for-action"

(11) Converting Features into Benefits

A feature is a distinct characteristic or a trait of an item, idea, product or person. For the sake of simplicity, I will refer to product "X" for illustration purposes. It could also be idea X or behavior X, however, to keep it simple, I will focus on features of a product. A feature (or set of features) of product X will help you define the product and the purpose of the product. It will clarify the product's niche. It will also help differentiate product X from a competitive product that may have been initially viewed as the same type of product. For example, if you are selling product X and you are competing with product "Y" (which basically does the same thing) you, as the salesperson or person attempting to be influential for any reason, must differentiate product X from product Y. Therefore, you should begin by illustrating the feature(s) of product X. For example, this Product X recording device has a fifty-gigabyte capacity.

The next important step involves converting the features of Product X into benefits. For example, I am demonstrating how you (the one I am attempting to persuade) will gain or profit from the feature(s) of product X. The same holds true if I am trying to influence a person to act a certain way; i.e., "To behave accordingly is beneficial because…" Essentially, The benefit is the advantage of an idea, item, product, conduct or person. The benefit should also be the differentiating factors of your product or idea. For example, the Product X recording device's *feature* is a fifty-gigabyte capacity, which allows you the *benefit* to record thousands of songs, and pictures along with many movies.

In order to convert a feature to a benefit, each feature should be supported with the answers to the following questions:

⇒ Why is this feature important? What is the value of the feature?
⇒ How will one gain or profit from using this feature?
⇒ What is the advantage to using these features?

See below for some more examples of how you can convert a feature into a benefit in your daily life. You will find this technique important no matter which hat you are wearing and no matter which task you are multi-tasking. Whether you are a professional, parent, mentor or customer, converting features into benefits will enable you to REACH Presentation Skills and inspire others.

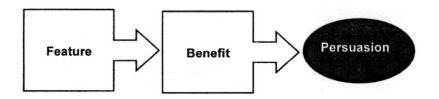

Feature: Product X is better than product Y because it has a longer handle.
Benefit: This will allow for greater torque thereby requiring less physical strain from you.

Feature: Your room is clean and organized.
Benefit: This will allow you to have much more room to play and study.

Feature: Monica is a better candidate for the job because of her wonderful attitude.
Benefit: She will add to, not take away from, our electrifying work environment.

Feature: Brionna's exercise plan consists of running and stretching.
Benefit: The plan will help you become stronger, healthier, and more flexible.

Feature: This new memory device has a capacity of 4 gigabytes.
Benefit: You can store much more data in this new device than your older 128-megabyte thumb drive.

Feature: This particular bank has more ATM machines throughout the state as it compares to any other Florida bank.
Benefit: More ATM machines equates to greater convenience to their customers.

Feature: The state college has a reputation as an academically top rated college.

Benefit: Its students will get a better education and, due to the school's reputation, the students will have more opportunities after they graduate.

Feature: This medicine works on a cellular level.

Benefit: It will increase efficacy while reducing potential adverse events.

Feature: This brand of sneaker has a thick sole, yet it has a feeling of lightness to it.

Benefit: The sneakers will protect your joints when you do high-impact exercises.

Feature: This watch is waterproof.

Benefit: You can take the watch into the water without damaging it.

(12) Seek Confirmation

Seek confirmation from the one you are attempting to persuade or influence. This is a critical element to the Power of Persuasion. This is no easy task to master. For one reason, most people do not like to be sold on something or, for that matter, be persuaded from their own ideology. If you are seeking confirmation, you are asking the person you are attempting to influence, if he or she understands the value of an idea or product as you understand its value. Imagine how much easier it is to close-for-action if your presentation was informative, convincing and intelligent enough to get the prospect to confirm that your product is valuable and/or an asset worth an investment. This is also true when it comes to an idea or a behavior.

Therefore, you must learn if you were able to convince the prospect or addressee that your idea or product is valuable. What good does it do to simply talk on and on mindlessly? It must be your objective to learn if the person you are attempting to influence understands the point or reasoning you are attempting to convey. Has your presentation identified a reason for the prospect to be persuaded? Was your presentation perceived by the addressee to be informative? As discussed above, did you probe and learn what features are important to the one to whom you are speaking and did you use that information during your presentation? Essentially, you must ask and seek confirmation from the addressee to learn the answer to those questions.

"The fool tells me his reasons,
The wise man persuades me with my own."
ARISTOTLE

How can you be sure whether or not you where persuasive? You need to first learn whether or not they agree with you and, therefore, understand the value of your product, position or idea as you understand its value. Once you have established agreement, then you can seek confirmation that your product, position or idea is an intelligent and optimal choice. If they agree and understand the value, you are prepared to gain commitment from them. In the sales profession, this next step is to close-for-action.

(13) Close-For-Action

Always close-for-action, that is, as long as you have earned the right.

Imagine the following setting: You are at your favorite restaurant, preparing to eat your favorite meal. In front of you, just below your nose, is a thick, juicy steak and it has the kind of aroma that is making your mouth water and your stomach gurgle. It is as if the sizzling steak is tantalizing your taste buds with the steam that is originating from it as it stretches up for your nostrils; you begin anticipating its robust, mouth-watering flavors. Just before you are about to sink your fork and knife into your luscious meal, you realize that you forgot to place the final ingredients on it. It is your personal touch that will separate your steak from every other steak in the restaurant. This personal touch is your preferred ratio of salt to pepper.

The only problem is, the saltshaker and peppershaker are at the other end of the table. Between you and the other end of the table is a group of people that you would consider mere acquaintances; adding to the level of difficulty, they are engaged in conversation. Consequently, you feel awkward and a bit reluctant to interrupt them.

"Boy, oh boy," you think to yourself, "I sure wish I didn't have to disturb all those people, but how else can I get the salt and pepper?"

Your mouth continues to produce more saliva in preparation for this great feast. Every last one of your nine thousand taste buds is ready to dance the salsa. The only problem is, you're not cutting into your steak. You are just gazing at the salt and pepper wishing both shakers would shake their way to you, via telepathy. Of course, neither the saltshaker nor the peppershaker make it your way and you find yourself generating enough courage to interrupt everyone at the table because your anticipation is too great.

Suddenly, you blurt out, "May I have the salt and pepper, please?" as if your mouth was just liberated from the rest of your body. Within a second, an eerie lull begins to hover over the table as everyone stops talking and looks at you. What happens next? The saltshaker and peppershaker are relayed from the opposite end of the table to you. As a result, you are able to enjoy your steak, just as you like it, all because you made the important decision to close-for-action. Simple, isn't it?

Closing-for-action could be that simple for you as well. It all depends on how much you want to enjoy your feast. Closing-for-action is simply asking someone to do something that you wish to be accomplished. Unfortunately, you are not going to inspire someone to do something just because you wish they would. Just like the saltshaker and peppershaker, you have to ask for it. As most of us have learned, mental telepathy does not work when we are trying to influence another or close-for-action.

How can you effectively close-for-action? First and foremost, you have to believe in your product, behavior or idea. If you truly believe in your product, behavior or idea, you will speak confidently, passionately and illustrate its value powerfully. Whenever I felt I demonstrated the value of my product to a prospect, as I understood its value, I felt extremely confident and comfortable closing-for-action. It is relatively easy to close a prospect when you believe the prospect understands the merit(s) of your product and is, therefore, persuaded. When is it difficult to close-for-action? When you did not have the time to do a good presentation or when your presentation was substandard. If you were not confident with the way you presented your product or idea, you will not likely feel confident when you attempt to close-for-action. This is the reason it is critical to prepare for your presentation. If you believe in your product or idea, you must take on the responsibility to be prepared to show others its true value. If the product is good, but your presentation is poor, you will fail to meet your objective because people will not understand its potential or value. Consequently, you have just done your idea, product, company, customer and/or child a disservice.

Thus, the ability to close-for-action at the end of the presentation or conversation is dependent upon your preparation, the very first moment you have established eye contact, said hello and every word uttered to the end of the conversation. Was the journey a smooth ride or were there too many obstacles that you could not overcome because of your lack of preparation and therefore, lack of commitment for accomplishing your goal?

In summary, if you inculcate the lessons within this book while you communicate with others, you should be in position to experience success as you confidently interact with others. If you are confident in your presentation, you will be more confident and able to close-for-action. Whenever I was confident in my product and I did a good presentation illustrating the features of my product to a customer, I could not fathom how the customer did not understand the value of my product as I understood it. I was self-assured to the point that the only rational conclusion was, "Clearly I have a remarkable product to offer!" This is a key component; you must believe in your product, or idea, and sell it with passion.

I once worked with a representative who presented her products with the kind of conviction that few could duplicate. Her name was Monica. By the time she finished presenting her product to her customers, she was convinced that her customers considered her product to be the best one available. This is the type of zeal that consistently elevated her sale's performance to the top of her company, every year. It was her enthusiasm for her product that differentiated her abilities from both her colleagues and competitors.

With that said, closing-for-action upon completion of a presentation or discussion, sounds relatively easy. In the end, all one needs to do is ask for the desired action. In comparison to all the other items to the Power of Persuasion, this appears to be the easiest. Perhaps, perhaps not, it truly depends on the effectiveness and the quality of your sales call, conversation or presentation.

Always close-for-action, that is, as long as you earned the right.

At this point of the chapter, you may have one of three thoughts about closing-for-action, which I address below:

A. To Close-for-action is a trivial matter

B. You may feel uncomfortable closing-for-action because you find it awkward for both you and the addressee and, therefore, you avoid it as if it were a pestilence

C. You may believe closing is such a "no-brainer" that even a child can master it without much effort and, therefore, you have no need to review how to close-for-action

A. To Close-For-Action is Trivial

"To Close-for-action is a trivial component of a presentation, conversation or discussion." This statement can be summed up with one straightforward word, wrong! What happens with a charming new cookie jar if you do not close it? The cookies become unpalatable. What happens to a state-of-the-art freezer if the door is not closed? The ice will melt. What happens to an oven that is set to bake at 375 degrees, however the door is not closed? The pie will never get done. What is your opinion on a book that has a story that you consider to be a captivating thriller throughout, until you reach its conclusion, which you consider to be poor? It ruins the entire book. What, then, would happen to a presentation that has no successful close? Chances are, nothing. No sale. No persuasion. No good ending. Essentially, closing-for-action is a critical component for your success. It is your conclusion to the story that you just told.

B. Awkwardness

The second aforethought has to do with a person's feelings of awkwardness as he attempts to close-for-action. This is a very real issue that many people grapple with upon most daily sales calls. In most situations, the problem is simply a lack of confidence. This issue can be rectified if you can pinpoint the problem, which is likely found in one of the following three areas:

⇒ The product/idea: If the product or idea is not good, it will be difficult to present it effectively and passionately because you won't believe in it yourself.

⇒ The nature/quality of the call: You may not have been able to present your product well because you kept getting interrupted or the addressee was simply not interested.

⇒ The salesperson/presenter: Lack of preparation, lack of training, new salesperson, or the lack of confidence in the product.

• *Addressing and resolving any one of the said mentioned issues gives you the potential to dispel the uncomfortable feelings of awkwardness.*

C. "…Even a Child Can Close"

To those who have children in their lives, marvel at the innate abilities, techniques and shameless tenacity of the master closers: our children. You want to learn how to close-for-action? Observe children. Having been blessed with the wonderful experience of fatherhood, I have seen, firsthand, my daughter close-for-action masterfully. Unfortunately, it was most often I who has been the recipient to her relentless closing techniques. Therefore, I have learned that even a child can (and will) master this technique, naturally. The reason children are experts in this area is simple: They are always (and I mean always) using and fine-tuning their closing methods; they are committed to and quite diversified in this skill set.

What follows is a sample of my daughter Brionna's thought process when she was three-and-a-half years old. Notice how she uses eight out of thirteen of the aforementioned Lucky 13 imperatives, rendering me, her father, defenseless:

(1) Brionna's Pre-call Plan

> **Brionna:** How can I persuade daddy to buy me this doll?

Well, firstly, after reviewing his history, I have learned that he loves me more than life itself, so I need to take advantage of this knowledge. Oh yes, he loves the title, "dada!" I must remember to include this title first, in my introduction and then throughout my presentation. This will contribute to the rapport I have established throughout our three-and-a-half year relationship.

Secondly, after reviewing past experiences, I seem to recall he is putty-in-my-hands every time I gaze into his eyes. Eye contact is critical. I need to be certain that just as he is about to look into my eyes and say 'no!' I open my eyes a little wider than normal. As a result, my big, green eyes will be in the right position to mesmerize him; for some reason, this technique is foolproof. It also contributes to the rapport building process.

Finally, I have just studied and reviewed the features of the doll and I must use that knowledge to educate him on those features and benefits during my presentation.

Oh, here comes daddy. It is time for me to implement the Power of Persuasion:

(2) Introduction

Brionna: I must begin with a hug and continue developing my rapport as well as get a feel for his mood

"I missed you today dada. Why did it take you so long to meet us at the mall?"

"Hello Brionna, I missed you as well. I know I'm late, I got delayed at work."

(3) Teach

(First stage of eye manipulation begins; the "gaze!")

"Dada, this doll is pretty, I love it because the color of her eyes are the same as mine...see!"

(4) Listening Skills

Brionna: This is where I am very impressive; I know exactly how to react depending on the way daddy (oh yeah, I mean…dada*)* responds to my request. Firstly, I must listen to the *way* in which he answers. If he tells me to put it back on the shelf, I will listen to the degree of sincerity in his voice when he tells me to, "put the doll back!" Secondly, I must listen to the words he uses. Are they words that will allow me to elaborate on the features of the doll or the cost of the doll? I must listen for his objections.

"No Brionna, we are not buying you anything today."

(5) Probes

"Why? What don't you like about the pretty doll with the big, green eyes…dada?"

[**My thoughts as Brionna's Father:** I assume my daughter wants to know if I can come up with a logical reason that she cannot have the doll so she will then attempt to overcome my objection (Just like a good salesperson; or is she just like her mother?)]

(6) Features and Benefits

"You see dada, not only are the eyes like mine but I can change her diapers. This will teach me what it is like to take care of a real baby. It will also keep me very busy while you are away on business trips."

(A hint of guilt will go a long way.)

(7) Seek Confirmation

"Dada, don't you agree that this is a pretty doll and it will keep me very busy while you are away on your business trips?"

(He is weakening, time to close-for-action)

"Well, I don't know Brionna, let me think about it. Didn't I just buy you a doll last month?"

(8) Close-For-Action

   Brionna: The timing on my eye manipulation technique is imperative (whatever that means). Here I go:

"Dada, will you buy me this doll today, please!"

(The gaze intensifies)

"Okay, but nothing else!"

He's putty-in-my-hand!

Children know how to close-for-action; they are both fearless and tenacious. If you have children, you can empathize. If you don't, the next time you are at a store, observe a child asking her mother or father for something; you are very likely going to learn about the technique of closing a prospect. Indeed, most children are fearless when it comes to closing. Why? Because they want "it" so much that their desire to have it far outweighs their fear of rejection. This desire creates that passion and tenacity.

Query: How badly do you want to succeed? How badly do you want to influence?

Fear of Rejection vs. Desire

If you put forth an abundance of energy throughout your presentation, why not put forth the same amount of energy during the close? Think about how often you have been on the border of some issue, or ambivalent about a purchase, and you simply walked away from it without taking the final step. Compare that to the times when someone was by your side (friend, salesperson, or facilitator) giving you just the right push to persuade you into something. You were more than likely influenced.

In essence, closing-for-action can make the difference with the Power of Persuasion. It is much like participating in a marathon. Your goal is to cross the finish line. What would you think of yourself if you ran a strong twenty-five-and-a-half miles, however you decided to simply stop one-half of a mile shy of the finish line for no apparent reason other than the lack of desire or the fear of finishing? Why race if you do not plan on finishing? Why would you initiate an action if you do not plan to meet your goal? You wouldn't. With all certainty, the same is true with a persuasive discussion as you attempt to be great and inspire.

"Based on our discussion, wouldn't you agree that the unique characteristics of the dolphin make it the most beautiful marine mammal that God has ever created?"

I can ask the above confidently because I believe my presentation consisted of many of the Lucky 13 elements that are within this chapter. By the way, it is labeled Lucky 13 because if you learn how to habitually use many, or all, of these thirteen aforesaid imperatives into your conversation or presentation, you will begin to believe you have the "luck of an Irishman" due to the variety of circumstances that begin to go your way. Try persuading someone without the use of many of the elements of Lucky 13. The chances are, you will be unable to meet your goal of being perceived as one who is informative or influential. You will be unable to cross the finish line.

You do not have to agree that the dolphin is the most beautiful marine mammal that God has ever created, however, notice how certain I am throughout the dissertation. Notice that I am not only confident with my level of knowledge, but also with the delivery of that knowledge, and that is a result of my due diligence. I am also confident in the product that I am presenting; the dolphin truly is a beautiful creature. Furthermore, notice how confident I am with the close. Indeed, my goal is persuasion, however, I am aware that I may not have persuaded everybody reading this chapter; nonetheless, should I persuade six out of ten readers, in the realm of sales, that is a profitable outcome.

With regard to profit, as you are speaking, consider that there is potential profit in every word you choose. With that said, you must also consider that there is potential loss in every word you choose. Therefore, choose wisely. In most anything we do, we have to communicate with people. Many times throughout the day, we must influence others (whether it is children, family, friends, employees, employers, strangers, or prospects). For this reason, you must read this chapter, learn from this chapter and practice continuously. You must learn how to use and incorporate all the steps of Lucky 13 in order to master the Power of Persuasion and REACH Presentation Skills so you can then be great and inspire. There is a caveat. You cannot read it once and expect to become an expert. Like everything else in life, you need to study and practice repeatedly. As you are conversing, be aware of these critical items. After awhile, like anything else you practice, it will become second nature to you, a habit.

To repeat Zig Ziglar from his book, *SECRETS OF CLOSING THE SALE*:

> *"When is it too early to close a sale? Too early is when you attempt to close before you have established in the prospect's mind significant value for what you are selling."*

Whether you are having a simple, informal conversation or if you are attempting to influence your child to the importance of living a life full of meaning, your communication skills can be a powerful vehicle. You will be more likely to reach your goals if you choose the right words and deliver those words, masterfully. Once you master these skills, you will realize that you have developed a sixth sense. This sixth sense will be similar to the dolphin's ability to sense its surroundings via echolocation. If you consider an issue between you and another party to be important, then you must learn to better understand the people with whom you are in communication. Indeed, this is not an easy task. You must develop your "echolocation" to be successful.

We may not have the same ability as a dolphin to sense another's state of mind, however, we do have an ability to develop a sixth sense. We can sense another person's emotional state just as a dolphin can determine another dolphin's emotional state; we just use our own unique skill sets. For example, dolphins have the innate ability to emanate burst-pulse sounds and interpret those sounds; while humans can listen, observe, process, understand and interpret another person's gestures and behaviors. By way of our experience, understanding, listening skills and through cognitive effort, a human can sense another's emotional state and then act accordingly. The components of Lucky 13 as well as the fundamental skills found in the Power of Conversation will help you develop your echolocation as you attempt to REACH Presentation Skills. So, be great and inspire.

SECTION THREE

3

SECTION THREE

The Power of
Presentation Skills

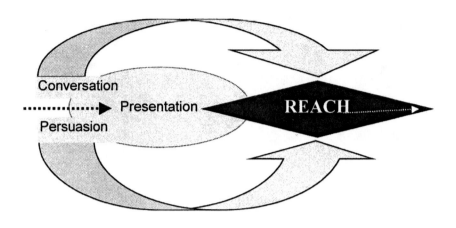

There is a very important word within the phrase, "presentation skills." At this point of the book, I imagine that one would immediately assume I am referring to the word, "presentation;" indeed, that is essentially the nature of this book. Interestingly, if that is your assumption, you are not correct. "Skills" is the word to which I am referring. When one refers to a skill, one must consider a process of development. One must consider the process that one must routinely go through, for various durations of time, which is necessary if one wishes to acquire specific proficiencies. You are not typically born with the fullest potential of a skill; you are born with potential to develop a God given ability. Whether or not you develop that skill to your fullest potential is entirely your responsibility. In other words, God makes you earn it. The question is, are you willing to take the necessary time and put forth the effort to earn the height of your potential?

With all certainty, we see professional athletes who clearly have natural advantages, i.e. size, strength, and speed. However, they have worked assiduously to further enhance their skills, which enable them to compete at such remarkable and rewarding levels. Thus, you may be born with an aptitude but you have to earn your skills if you want to successfully compete in life.

The same must be said when one is referring to the skill of

presenting. This fact is intuitive, yet most people simply don't practice this important skill. Sure, we understand the importance of practicing our golf swing over and over again. We can accept the importance of practicing a musical instrument daily so we can hit the right notes at the right time. We can even comprehend the reasoning for target practice as we seek the tip of an arrow to meet the center of a target some distance away. Yet, when it comes to presenting something of value, we take it for granted that the first time we stand up to present our material, we will perform at our highest level. A level, we presume, which would be synonymous to the effort that was put into the content of the presentation itself. Unfortunately, just like shooting a bow-n-arrow, we may clearly see our target when we begin the presentation, but we will miss our target lock, stock and barrel without the necessary practice and preparation. The reason is simple; there is no effective "presentation" without the "skills." In short, to develop a skill, one must practice.

I have seen this mistake over and over again. People spend hours, days even months on a PowerPoint presentation and then they stand up for the first time in front of their target audience, and fumble through it because they didn't invest the necessary time to practice. The material, data or content within the presentation is typically good, well thought out, even supported by years of research, yet, the audience will completely miss the point of the slide or set of slides simply due to poor preparation on the part of the presenter. In fact, there are certain situations when this may be analogous to a football team. The owner of the team spends millions of dollars recruiting coaches and players who in turn spend countless hours reviewing film, drawing up plays and going though innumerable repetitions of physical exercises. It all becomes futile if the quarterback fails to execute the designed plays on the day of the game because he didn't take the time to practice.

A presenter must take the time to practice the presentation. As a result of his due diligence, his dialogue will be more concise, the transitions from one idea to another will be smooth and he will be a presenter whose confidence is apparent. These actions will create a momentum that will cause enjoyment for, not only the presenter, but also his audience. The people to whom he presents will find that the presentation glides forward with surprising ease. Without the necessary preparation, he will probably struggle and it will become obvious to the audience. Compare it to a bird in flight. When a bird is flying in the same direction that a strong wind is blowing, the bird flies gracefully, effortlessly, and brilliantly. When that same bird does a one hundred and eighty degree turn and flies against the wind, it flies inelegantly, unwieldy and stressfully.

In order to REACH Presentation Skills, one must practice; after all, it is a skill. Think about it, what skill is there that doesn't require some type of practice? I remember a kinesiology class I once took in high school. We had to learn how to juggle. The purpose was to become aware of how the body slowly learns to make certain movements automatic. Our bodies adapt to repetitive movements. This is accomplished slowly, over much time and repetition. For the first week, I continuously dropped the balls; I was clumsy. After awhile, however, something interesting happened; I slowly learned how to juggle. What I once thought was impossible, slowly became possible.

The same is true with presenting in front of an audience. At first it is intimidating but if you learn how to slowly become comfortable articulating the content of your presentation, the words that you are using will flow naturally. The process of exchanging one word for another becomes automatic as you learn to successfully present, just as it becomes automatic to exchange one ball for another as you learn to successfully juggle. Before you know it, you are choosing words and phrases with discretion in conjunction with a masterful delivery. Your exchanges become steady, smooth, and confident as you go from one word to the next. It is at this point that you create a momentum as you deliver your words masterfully, greatly, and inspirationally.

What follows, is a set of important guidelines that you should implement during a presentation. Also, consider many of the aforementioned important skills from the Power of Conversation and the Power of Persuasion. These imperatives will prepare you to REACH Presentation Skills.

(1) Be Yourself

> *Surely you desire truth in the inner parts;*
> *You teach me wisdom in the inmost place.*
> PSALM 51:6

I lead with this imperative because, just as in the Power of Conversation, you are not you, without you, as you REACH Presentation Skills. Simply, the optimal identity that you should exhibit when you present to others is your own. You shouldn't attempt to emulate someone else. If you don't remain true to yourself, you are not being true to your audience. Inevitably, your audience will see you as a fake and this will cost you something that is difficult to regain; i.e., trust. You cannot effectively present if you are less than natural; thus, be true to your audience by being true to yourself.

Each one of us is unique. Some of us have yet to find that special set of qualities. Others have found their 'one of a kind' style but are not sure how to comfortably express it, particularly when they attempt to present in front of an audience. Often, people realize this discomfort and try to settle their anxiety by consciously or unconsciously imitating someone else whom they consider skillful. This tactic of trying to imitate someone else's behaviors, mannerisms or style is a common mistake. You have to trust the person that you are and realize that your unique qualities are beautiful. Bring out your traits as if they are toys in a box that you have decided to share with your friends. What you will find is that you will make others more comfortable and, therefore, more willing to share their toys. This manifestation is trust. Remember, you are not you, without you.

(2) Practice the Presentation

As mentioned above, presenting is a skill, an acquired skill, which must be practiced just as any other skill must be practiced. For example, law students don't just stick their nose in a book during their minimum of three years of law school; they practice their presentation skills. They are put in front of a mock court, mock judge and mock jury and practice this very useful skill. They have to REACH Presentation Skills because one day, many of the law students may find themselves fighting for millions of dollars in a lawsuit. Others may very likely be deliberating for an innocent person's freedom. Therefore, law students spend countless hours improving on their presentation skills.

You may not be fighting for millions of dollars or deliberating for a person's freedom, but if you are in front of an audience, you have a responsibility to practice before you stand up and present. It is through repetition that you will REACH Presentation Skills. Like everything else in life, you have to go out and earn it; it is purely your responsibility.

(3) Know Your Audience

In keeping with the law analogy, before a trial takes place, lawyers attempt to get to know the jury; which, essentially, is an audience who the lawyers want to influence or persuade. They go through a painstaking process of jury selection by asking each potential juror a set of questions. The intent is for the attorneys to become more familiar with each jury candidate, who are part of a large pool of candidates. As they get more familiar with the large number of candidates, the attorneys will then be able to whittle down the candidates to a select few, who will ultimately be selected as members of the jury. The remaining candidates get dismissed. By the end of the jury selection procedure, the attorneys for both parties will likely know the jury. This will enable them to present with a certain style, touch certain emotions and be influential in one capacity or another.

The aforesaid point is also important to anybody who is going to present to an audience. As mentioned in the previous chapter, the Power of Persuasion, you should not only have a general understanding of your audience's expectations, you should also know what is important to them. You have to focus on those specific items to effectively inspire your audience. You should also try to establish a rapport with your audience prior to the presentation. If the audience is a reasonable size, you can introduce yourself as many or all of them are walking in. Go up to them and make small talk. Get familiar with your audience at some level. This approach will help you get more comfortable with your audience and your audience more comfortable with you. Suddenly you are no longer a stranger to your audience. If you consider a presentation as a conversation, then you realize the importance of establishing a rapport or a comfort level. This approach will help you REACH Presentation Skills and become inspirational.

It is important to note that when you are presenting your material or ideas, you are attempting to persuade them. You want them to see and understand the materials or ideas as you do. You, essentially, want to inspire your audience. This is persuasion. If you wish to accomplish this mission, you must be willing to put forth an effort that goes beyond just standing in front of your audience and pointing to images or data on a screen. You are less likely to be successful with that lackluster approach. Therefore, you have to use many of the techniques discussed in the previous chapter. As with everything else in life, you have to be willing to earn your success. You have to be willing to earn your skills to present effectively.

(4) Be Responsible to Your Audience (The "3 E's" of Responsibility)

If an audience is going to sit and exchange their time for your presentation, you have a responsibility to that audience; act accordingly. Treat this often overlooked fact as biblical truth. Just as your time is valuable to you, their time is equally valuable to them. Just as you expect your audience to respect you as you are presenting, give them the respect they deserve as they take the time to listen. Just as it could be uncomfortable presenting, it could be equally uncomfortable listening. Therefore, assume a responsibility to your audience with the "3 E's" of presenter responsibility. Assume the responsibility to educate, entertain and excite your audience.

⇒ Educate with accurate information. Do your research.
⇒ Entertain your audience with the skills mentioned in this book. Consider taking a short acting class. This will help you learn to be more comfortable and confident

presenting in front of others. You will also learn to be more expressive.

⇒ Excite your audience by presenting information that is important to them and do so in an interesting manner. In other words, present with passion.

(5) Maintain Eye Contact

While presenting, it is important to make a "connection" with your audience. This technique is consistent with the first chapter, the Power of Conversation. If you can make a connection with your audience during a presentation, similar to making a connection with an individual during a one-on-one conversation, your presentation is more likely going to be considered a success. The ability to maintain eye contact in both situations is critical to that success. This skill will help you build a rapport with your audience, one person at a time.

There is something intimate and natural about this non-verbal exchange. Notice when babies look your way; once they become aware of you, they typically look straight into your eyes. This exchange will ingenuously create a smile from both the baby and you. In fact, even animals tend to look at us in the eyes. Therefore, to maintain eye contact in many scenarios is natural and it is expected; that is certainly the case during a presentation. This technique takes confidence, which can only be developed with practice. Finally, maintaining eye contact is important for another reason. Not only does it get the audience more comfortable with you, it will help you become more comfortable with your audience.

(6) Understand (and Believe in) Your Material

Just as it is important to practice the material that you are going to present, you have to prepare by thoroughly reviewing and understanding the material. This statement appears instinctive, however, it is surprising how often people don't take the time to learn the material as well as they should. When this situation occurs it truly is a waste of the audience's time. Moreover, the presenter should feel shame because this manifestation is simply a result of laziness and may be perceived as an act of indifference. Therefore, illustrate your sincerity by understanding the material so you can articulate it in a comprehensive fashion. If you must use notes as a reference, do so discretely. In other words, don't rely on your notes to get you through the presentation; only use them as a reference. Refer to them occasionally. Use them as a guide to help you recall main points however, you should understand the nuances of your presentation so you can deliver it confidently and masterfully.

Unfortunately, there is no magic trick to learning the material. You have to put in the time to study what you are going to present. The better you understand the background information that supports your presentation, the more self-assured you will be with your presentation. You will also be more confident during the question and answer section of your presentation.

Another important symptom to understanding the material is that you will truly believe in the material that you are planning to present. There is no faking this important item. If you believe in the nuances of your presentation, you will very likely present it with passion. Subsequently, the audience will presumably recognize your passion and believe you are genuine. Believing in your material will help you inspire others, therefore, take the necessary time to learn and understand the details of your material; it will be well worth it for both your audience and you.

What follows are a few tips to presenting informatively:

⇒   Take the necessary time to study and review the background information of each illustration

⇒   If the illustration has a graph with an x-axis and y-axis, review separately, what the y-axis represents and then the x-axis. Get familiar with the graph by breaking it into parts and then verbally rebuild it for your listener(s). This will take some effort, however, as the presenter, it is your responsibility to clarify what you are presenting. Be aware that most people listening will not put forth the necessary effort to elucidate complicated charts or illustrations for themselves. It is the presenter's responsibility.

⇒ Use mnemonics, which is a method used to assist your memory to recall important information. For example, if you are planning to present the history of jazz, and you want to discuss the order of the music alphabet, you could easily remember its correct order using mnemonics. To illustrate: There are seven notes that get placed on a staff, which comprise of five horizontal lines and four spaces on sheet music. To remember the piano notes that are placed on the lines for your right hand, known as the treble staff, which is the musical staff carrying the treble clef, use the following mnemonic: "**E**very **G**ood **B**oy **D**oes **F**ine." This phrase represents the following notes in the treble clef in its proper ascending order: E, G, B, D, and F. Regarding the notes that are placed on the spaces, simply spell F.A.C.E.
Another example of a mnemonic would be if you are discussing the cardiovascular system and you have a difficult time remembering the blood flow. Remember that the "a" in artery stands for "away," as in the following: The blood in the arteries flows *away* from the heart.

⇒ Practice your transitions from one topic, slide or illustration to the next. The more you practice, the better able you are to anticipate and smoothly make transition. This technique in itself is an art form.

⇒ If you are uncertain about some type of information, concede to someone in the audience or to the one to whom you are speaking. It is better to admit that you don't know, or admit that you are speculating, rather than to misinform others. Once you lose your credibility, it is difficult to regain.

⇒ Prior to your presentation, collaborate with, and gain confirmation from, somebody who is an expert in the area of your topic.

⇒ Practice the actual articulation of your presentation many times. Your mind may have it while your mouth may not.

(7) Fluctuate Your Voice

According to Merriam-Webster on-line dictionary, the word monotone is defined as "a succession of syllables, words, or sentences in one unvaried key or pitch." It happens when someone is speaking without concern for his or her voice fluctuation. In short, there is no rise or fall in one's voice. It is as bad as a person attempting to perform a song but by using only one note to perform that song. The reason such a song has never been recorded is because nobody wants to listen to it. With all certainty, the same conclusion can be made regarding a lecturer with a monotone voice or an extremely narrow range; no one wants to listen because, frankly, such a lecture would be quite boring regardless of the material.

Your voice is the vehicle that is delivering your message so inspire others by choosing the right words with a masterful delivery. Speak with authority and fluctuate your voice while you are speaking. Learn to raise your voice to emphasize certain words or phrases. Change the notes in your voice as you attempt to differentiate one phrase from another. Practice the articulation of your presentation so you know which words and phrases you want to underscore with your voice.

If you consider your message to be important, then consider the delivery of your message to be equally important. If you don't, you will fail to get your message across and you will have wasted a lot of time and energy. However, if you take the time to prepare for your presentation as a singer prepares her song, you will engage your audience because your delivery will be masterful.

(8) Project Your Voice (Become larger than the screen)

Speak with passion in your voice and demonstrate to your audience that you know what you are talking about. The ability to project your voice will demonstrate your confidence in the material. It will also keep your audience engaged. A simple technique that you can use is to speak to the last row of your audience. This is especially important if you are not using a microphone. Look at the person at the most remote area of the room and raise your voice as if you are addressing only that person. Depending on the size of the room, you may feel as if you are being too loud. Although this appears to be true to you, the opposite is more likely true to the audience. This is one reason it is important to practice and find the right volume level prior to your presentation.

If possible, I recommend that you go early and ask a friend to sit in the back of the room and then address that person. Ask your friend if he or she can comfortably hear you. At that point, you will learn the appropriate volume and how best to project your voice. Remember, it will often feel like you're too loud; however, to the persons in the last few rows of the room, you will likely sound just right and to the people in the first few rows, you will sound strong and confident.

(9) Your Positioning

Your positioning is very important when you present in front of an audience. It is important to find a point on the floor that puts you in an area of command by not putting yourself in a position that will create distractions. Note that there are only a few critical areas on the floor/stage that will help you realize a commanding presence, which also means that there are many areas on the floor/ stage that may cause you to falter, wallow or fail. For example, if you are presenting with the use of a projector, do your absolute best to never walk between the projector and the screen, especially while you are speaking. If you do, you will have images appear on your head, torso or, worst of all, lower body areas. This is very distracting to your audience and is an unnecessary incident. It does not add to, but takes away from, your presentation.

Furthermore, if you are too far away from the screen for an extended period of time, your audience will be too focused on the images on the screen and not at all on you. As a result, you have relinquished a certain amount of stage presence; essentially, you have taken yourself out of the picture. In the latter scenario, you have made the screen the focal point of the presentation. To truly have an effective presentation, you should have a certain level of charisma and create a presence that is bigger than your screen. You won't be able to develop a rapport with your audience if they are too focused on the screen and not at all on you. This is the reason you have to consider all the elements in this book as you prepare for your presentation.

(10) Stand in One Place (it is not a Dance)

Speaking of unnecessary distractions, don't dance as you present. In other words, keep your feet planted firmly and confidently as you present; make just a few infrequent but specific steps and pivots. The unremitting nervous foot movements are common mistakes. People get anxious and create all kinds of their own distractions via gestures and body movements. Some people do the box step, some rock from left foot to right foot, others tap their feet and others stick to the traditional back and forth pacing routine. Save the dance steps for the dance floor. When you present, present with confidence and poise because unnecessary and troubling movements are distractions to the audience.

For example, I was at a seminar with over two thousand people in attendance. The venue was a sizeable ballroom. They had cameras in the back of the room aimed at the presenters on stage. Along the walls of each side of the stage were large screens. In the center wall, up stage, just behind the speaker, was another large screen. These screens were positioned high relative to the stage such that none of the members of the audience's view were obstructed. In other words, if one could not see the speaker on stage, one could simply look up at one of the three large screens. Regarding the scenery, the stage background had an extremely busy black and white pattern; almost like an enormous paisley tie.

As one of the main speakers presented, she started to pace incessantly; five steps to the left, then five steps to the right. The camera followed the speaker back and forth, back and forth. After a few minutes, I noticed that people started to look away from the large screens and began rubbing their eyes. Subsequently, many of them started to chatter softly amongst themselves. At first I didn't understand the reason, but then it became apparent; as they were looking at the screens, they were getting dizzy. While the speaker was pacing back and forth, five steps to the left then five steps to the right, etc., the busy black and white paisley patterns that filled the background of the stage, appeared to be set in a hectic motion on the screens, thus inducing a visually toxic affect to the spectators. Her pacing continued for twenty minutes; five steps left then five steps right. The more she paced, the dizzier her audience became; she, therefore, lost the audience who she was attempting to inspire.

The point is, I don't remember what she was presenting however I do remember the self-inflected distraction. Essentially, if the material is worth presenting, make it worth remembering; you owe it to your audience. Finally, save the dance steps for the dance floor and stand firmly and confidently. When you do decide to make movements, make them limited, decisive and deliberate.

(11) Laser Pointer: The P.A.R. Technique

The use of a laser pointer is a popular and necessary tool when one uses visual aides to present. Indeed, utilizing this tool to underscore an area on the screen is a preferred choice in comparison to walking up to the screen and pointing to it with your finger. Even though the latter scenario is intuitively wrong, invariably, people do it. One issue with walking up to the screen and using your finger is that you will place your body between the projector and the screen, thus placing images on your person. As mentioned in imperative number nine, this creates an unnecessary distraction. Another issue with walking up to the screen and pointing to it with your finger is that you will have to put your back to the audience as you speak toward the screen thereby creating a host of other concerns.

Clearly, the use of a laser pointer does create a more professional image. With that said, the use of such tools is not without its own set of rules; and where there are rules, there are sure to be pitfalls. One potential pitfall that often occurs with the use of laser pointers is that people don't use them properly. The most common error is when presenters use it to encircle a word, number, image or phrase that they wish to highlight. Once the presenter sets the red dot in a continuous circular motion, the audience's eyes and heads are soon to follow, in unison. They don't look at the context and, in its stead, become distracted by the circulating dot on the screen.

Another common mistake that presenters make with a laser pointer is that they turn their backs to the audience, point to a word, number, image or phrase on the screen and continue talking toward the screen. In this scenario, the issue is that the presenter is no longer engaged with the audience, via eye contact and voice projection. This is unnecessary. You don't gain anything from this maneuver.

While using a laser pointer put into practice, what I term, the "P.A.R." technique (Pause-Aim-Reengage):

⇒ **Pause**
⇒ Turn your head toward the screen
⇒ Find the word, number, image or phrase that you wish to highlight
⇒ Aim and point with the laser pointer
⇒ Release and turn back toward your audience
⇒ **R**eengage your audience with commentary

Your audience will perceive you as confident, knowledgeable and well prepared if you learn how to effectively use the P.A.R. Technique. Admittedly, pausing while you are in front of an audience is difficult. When you are the one who is conducting the presentation, it appears as if a few seconds of silence in front of an audience is more like a few minutes in front of a firing squad, with the aim directly on you. This is particularly true if you are not routinely presenting to an audience.

In truth, a pause adds to your presentation because it interrupts any set pattern that you may have in your voice. It also allows you the opportunity to reengage your audience. Think of it as reloading, which will enable you to refocus on your audience. Of course, if you do find that your audience turns into a firing squad because they don't agree with your presentation, a pause may be just what you need to find the right words that will keep them from firing a shot directly at you.

(12) Make Your Visual Aides, Visually Appealing

When you use a variety of approaches to learn something of value, you have the ability to use different parts of your brain and you, therefore, have greater potential for retaining that information. In other words, the more senses that are involved in your learning progression, the more you take advantage of the segments, or various lobes, of your brain. This expanded utility of your brain aides you with greater retention; this is a scientific fact.

For example, the frontal lobes are responsible for your motor skills, memory abilities, and impulse control. Located in the side of your head, above our ears, is your temporal lobe. This section of the brain processes the information that allows you to hear. It is also, to a lesser degree, responsible for memory and visual interpretation. When you see objects, you use the occipital lobe, which is posterior, located in the back of your brain. The detection of simple visual stimuli occurs in this part of the brain. Indeed, complex processing occurs within the occipital lobe. Interestingly, as stated by some scientists who study the brain, approximately half of the human brain is dedicated, in some capacity, to vision.

Visual learning is a proven teaching technique in which ideas, problems and concepts are linked with images and are represented graphically. [5] Additionally, it has been verified by various studies, that we are able to retain much more information when we learn audibly and visually versus audibly alone. People are able to associate images that are relevant to the data or text and, subsequently, recall those images. Visuals have the ability to touch people's emotions and when you touch people's emotions you have greater ability to teach someone something of value. Therefore, it stands to reason that visual aides are very important when you are attempting to influence, inform or inspire another.

Visual aides also make the presentation more enjoyable and people love to be entertained in this manner. This is one reason the home video market is a multi-billion dollar market, annually. This is also the reason that the television has become ubiquitous. As reported by

Nielsen Media Research, by 1998 ninety-eight percent of American homes had one or more television sets within it. Moreover, the 1940's, 50's and 60's illustrated that we prefer to listen to, as well as watch the images of, a story on television rather than simply listen to the same story on a radio broadcast.

As my former professor claimed, "A picture is worth 'more than' a thousand words." It is true that he expanded on an old cliché, but no one can rationally argue against this statement. For example, which lesson would have greater impact: A physician explaining the reasons why a person should quit smoking cigarettes; or a physician showing a picture of a black, rigid, necrotic lung as it compares to a picture of a nice, fresh, pink, healthy lung and then explaining the cause and affect of cigarettes on that black lung. In addition, a physician can show pictures of patients who once smoked, who are now committed to a breathing apparatus for the remainder of their fragmented lives.

Another example of learning via images is the skin specialist, the dermatologist. Pictures of skin and associated diseases of the skin stimulate them; this is how they are trained. In fact, much of their learning occurs by studying images of the skin. I remember a lunch conference I attended with a group of dermatologists. As the speaker was presenting data on the screen, the dermatologists would look down and reach for his or her food. When the speaker transitioned to a picture, all the dermatologists would look back up at the screen. As soon as the speaker changed to the next slide, which had more data, they would, in unison, look down at their meal and continue eating. It looked choreographed because it was consistent throughout the presentation. Data, look down and eat; image of skin, look up with interest.

People respond to images because images are stimulating to the brain. To go one step further, it can be argued that an image is important but not as important as a visually appealing image. Another scientific fact is that people are attracted to beauty. This is the reason advertisers are quick to use beautiful people in their advertisements.

It is difficult to argue against scientific facts but it is even more difficult when those facts are supported by common sense.

Presumably, many of the aforementioned scientifically established facts didn't surprise you; they seem plausible enough. Therefore, logic dictates that you should make your visual aides, visually appealing. It will help keep your audience focused and engaged by keeping them entertained and further stimulated; which may cause them to become inspired.

What follows are a few guidelines that you should consider as you prepare and enhance your presentation:

⇒ Select a nice background and appropriate slides
⇒ Use relevant pictures
⇒ Use relevant Clip Art
⇒ Use proper slide formatting
⇒ Font should be at least 36 (whenever possible)
⇒ Don't make the presentation into an eye chart (via small text)
⇒ Avoid busy slides (whenever possible)
⇒ Use interesting but relevant quotes
⇒ Spend time with the slide transitions
⇒ Work on word and picture animation to underscore main ideas

As obvious as this sounds, many people don't consider the relevance of enhancing the appearance of their presentation. There are many reasons for this oversight: they don't think about it; they don't consider it important; they don't want to take the time to do it; or they simply don't know how to enhance the appearance of their presentation.

For all intents and purposes, you must take the time to enhance the appearance of your presentation or have someone who knows how to make the enhancements for you. If you do, it will be obvious to your audience that you put forth the extra effort and they will appreciate it, whether consciously or unconsciously. The scientific facts support these important points. Lastly, your extra effort will likely make your presentation more enthusiastic and fun to communicate.

(13) Create Interesting, Informative and Creative Handouts

Whenever possible (depending on the topic being presented, the purpose of the presentation and the amount of people in the audience), it is nice to have creative and informative handouts available for reference purposes. It is helpful for two primary reasons. First, some people like to be able to follow along with a presentation via note taking. Having access to and taking notes on a handout is very convenient for many people. As illustrated in imperative number twelve, people learn in a variety of ways, therefore some people will benefit from a handout.

The second reason is that people will retain only a certain percentage of the information you are communicating. To make matters worse, unfortunately, the percentage of information retained, gets lost with time. Information that was once stored in the hippocampus, which is responsible for short-term memory, will probably be forgotten if it is not reinforced. This is one reason advertisements encourage you to "call now" at the end of the commercial. They know that with the elapsing of time, you are less likely to call and make a purchase. Having a handout available will reinforce your message and improve the chances that those who take the time to review it, will be able to retain the context of your message for a longer period of time compared to those who don't.

In addition to the thirteen imperatives listed above, what follows is a summary table of do's and don'ts. You will truly enhance your abilities, REACH Presentation Skills and inspire others, if you learn and practice the "do's," while deliberately avoiding the "don'ts."

Summary of Do's Do:	Summary of Don'ts Don't:
⇒ Be Yourself	⇒ Read the screen
⇒ Practice	⇒ Put back to your audience
⇒ Know your audience	⇒ Read notes continuously
⇒ Be responsible to your audience (Use the 3 "E's")	⇒ Move back and forth, pace or dance
⇒ Eye contact	⇒ Say, "This slide says…"
⇒ Really understand your material/believe in it. Use mnemonics.	⇒ Make screen focal point by excluding yourself
⇒ Fluctuate your voice	⇒ Use pointer as a conductor wand
⇒ Speak larger than the screen	⇒ Read/write every word on the slide
⇒ Be aware of your positioning on stage/ floor	⇒ Use small font
⇒ Stand in one place (No dancing, or pacing)	⇒ Take a deep breath, exhale and continue in a monotone voice
⇒ Point using P.A.R. technique	⇒ Use filler sounds like "ummm" or filler words or phrases like, "Ya know!"
⇒ Make your presentation visually appealing	⇒ End the presentation by saying, "and that is our presentation" or "that's it!"
⇒ Interesting/relevant handouts	⇒ Be a clown

⇒ Get audience participation (when relevant/appropriate). Engage	⇒ Chew gum/eat food
⇒ Dress appropriately	⇒ Use inappropriate language
⇒ Smile, have fun and engage	⇒ Walk past the first row and talk with your back to them
⇒ Creative slide show and transitions	⇒ Use words that you don't understand or be pompous
⇒ Font should be at least 36	⇒ Be afraid to say "I will have to get back with you on that question," if you don't know the answer
⇒ Repeat any questions asked by an audience member so everyone can hear the question and participate in the answer	⇒ Walk in front of the screen thereby having images on forehead, torso, or lower extremities

The skills to communicate and present to others are indeed unique skills because not enough people take the time to practice nor do they understand the relevance of practicing. One must consider the following: if an audience has agreed to take the time to listen to your presentation, then you must consider this opportunity as a sincere privilege. You must feel honored and with that comes a responsibility; the responsibility that you have towards your audience. If people agree to take the time to listen to your presentation, you are obligated to those people to go above and beyond their expectations. You have to accept the fact that you have a lot riding on your presentation. Whether it is your product, company, idea, or behaviors you are trying to change, or simply your reputation, the manner in which you choose to present (and represent) can either enhance or destroy it. This thought should motivate you to strengthen your skills by practicing the thirteen previously mentioned imperatives within this chapter.

Also, take the time to watch politicians on television. They have gone through rigorous communication and presentation skills training. This training is vital because their livelihood, reputation and a lot of money are dependent upon their performances. Once a politician walks on a stage he or she is placed at the media forefront, therefore, there is very little room for even one mistake. The zone of tolerance is quite narrow. For some reason, "we the people" anticipate a politician's next blunder. Invariably, the politicians for the opposing party will be more than happy to exploit those errors in judgment as well. This is one reason they work diligently to become polished with the hopes of being flawless. Notice their techniques and how they incorporate their unique style as they present. Additionally, learn from the politicians who have not acquired this important skill but are under the illusion that they have. You will notice what they are doing incorrectly and that will be a fun lesson within itself. In short, take the time to watch and learn from them. Politicians are always on one television station or another. This is a wonderful way for you to get free training at any time of the day or night.

Moreover, you can get the same type of free training by watching the innumerable news broadcasters who are on countless news stations throughout the day and night. Newscasters and sportscasters are generally very skilled and you can learn just by watching them. You can also learn from their mistakes and get a chuckle from it. The same is true as you are sitting in an audience during a presentation. Watch and learn from the presenter. Noticing his or her skills (or lack thereof) becomes intuitive. Determine for yourself what the presenter is doing well and in which areas he or she is in need of improvement. Lastly, you can learn by watching your priest, preacher or minister, as they deliver their sermon. Many of them have become quite skilled due to their experiences. One of their many responsibilities is to stand up in front of the parishioners and deliver a message. They do this numerous times a week, year after year and, therefore, have learned how to deliver their message masterfully.

The point is that we all have the ability to be great and inspire much in the way a myriad of others have been inspirational in the past, and will continue to do so in the future. Paul, the Apostle to the Gentiles, is proof that you can inspire an entire planet throughout millenniums with strong communication skills and leading by example. Fortunately, nobody expects us to mimic Paul's level of accomplishments, however, we all, on a smaller scale, do have the potential to affect lives for the better. God gives this awesome potential to us, via, the tools He provides each one of us. The caveat is that these tools, our brain and ability to communicate, give us only the potential. It is up to each of us to exploit those tools for the better by strengthening them and then utilizing them for inspiration. Like every other skill, we have to work diligently to improve.

May the words of my mouth and the meditation of my heart be pleasing in your sight, O Lord, my Rock and my Redeemer.
Psalm 19:14

Communication Through Action
(Are You More Likely to Inspire or Insult Another?)

Finally, I'd like to address communication and how it truly relates to parents, mentors and teachers. As mentioned above, inspiration doesn't have to be on a magnificent scale (like Paul's accomplishments) to be magnanimous. Are you magnanimous and do you inspire others to be magnanimous?

It is easier to understand these two questions if you fully understand the meaning of this uncommonly used word, magnanimous. It is Latin in origin; the first part of the word, *magnus*, is translated into English as *great*. The second part of the word, *animus*, is translated into English as *soul*. Thus, one who is magnanimous is one who has a great soul. Webster's New World Dictionary further defines the word magnanimous as one who is generous in overlooking injury or insult; rising above pettiness; and one who is noble. To be considered noble, one would be a person with high moral qualities. With this elaboration of the word, you can clearly see that you don't have to change the world to act magnanimously. You do, however, have to lead by example, if you wish to inspire others to act magnanimously. Therefore, I ask once again, are you magnanimous and do you inspire others to be magnanimous?

To consider why these two questions are significant to this book, think back to your childhood when you were quite impressionable. Were you repeatedly inspired or insulted by the people who influenced your life? This involves some thought. You may have an urge to immediately consider the insults first, because we often focus on the negative aspects of people's behaviors and comments that are directed towards us. For some reason, words of degradation dig deeper than words of praise. Think about those times, put it into its proper perspective and then put more thought into this question. Perhaps with more thought, you will recall the many inspirational events to which you were witness. What did these events and actions in your life communicate to you?

First, recall a time when an adult made a less than noble impression on you; an impression that you sensed at the time, and now interpret as, an act of wrongdoing or foul play. The act was nothing too malicious, but a moral transgression nonetheless. For example, you decided as a child that you would grow into a law-abiding person. You would be good to others and live by the "golden-rule." One day, when you were a sixteen-year-old stock clerk at a local grocery supermarket, you found a woman's purse in a parking lot inside a shopping cart. Apparently, as a woman was taking groceries out of the cart and placing them into her car, she left her purse behind. You decided that the right thing to do at that time was to take the purse up to your store manager so when the woman came back, she would be able to retrieve her purse, contents intact. This was an admirable act and you felt good about it, especially when the woman came up to you with relief on her face and gratitude in her heart. When you got home and proudly informed your father of your good deed, your father started to yell at you; "Are you crazy! Today is Saturday; the woman probably just cashed her paycheck. You could have had some money to put towards a car!" All you remember is your father's disappointment as he walked away from you.

Now, recall a moment in your childhood when an adult made a noble impression on you; an impression that you sensed at the time, and now interpret as, an act of goodness and kindness. This act was an act of selflessness. For example, think back to when you were a twelve-year-old. It was a cool summer evening and your father abruptly interrupted your sleep. As he rushed you out of the house, you noticed that the next-door neighbor's house was ablaze. Once your father delivered you to another neighbor for safekeeping, you saw him rush into the burning house. Five minutes later you witnessed him calmly and heroically walking out of the smoke filled doorway with your neighbor's child safely in his arms.

Both events are from my past and reside in my memory. Which of the two actions did I pull from as I transformed from a child into a man? By which action was I most influenced? What were my father's daily actions communicating to his impressionable son? Although this book is not a psychology book, it is important to think about these events because we, as adults, are communicating to our children by way of our actions. My father was both a good and, at times, a poor role model for his children. Most of the time, however, he had a positive impact on my young life and the lives of others.

Those were the actions for which I chose to influence my life as I grew up. Indeed, we do have this choice.

To expand, my father and mother were always around their children and verbalized the importance of an education and being respectful towards others. They also taught us the importance of family and that it was acceptable for a father to show his affection for his children. Showing affection may not sound important and when I was a boy, I didn't think much about it because my family has an Italian ancestry; kissing hello and goodbye was a part of our family culture.

But then one day, thirty years later, something interesting happened. Out of nowhere, I received a phone call from my childhood best friend, to whom I have not spoken in many years. His name is Dan. We were always together playing one type of sport or another. Well, at the time of the phone call, we were forty-year-old men with families of our own. After speaking for a while and getting caught up on the people, work and events that form each of our life, he told me something that brought a chill to run down my spine. He mentioned that he was never and is still not close to his father. I could hear the regret in his voice. His father never gave him any affection and that was fine with him as a child because that was his norm; he didn't know any other way of behavior. That is until one day, my father communicated an action that would help him with his children's rearing, twenty-five years later. Dan was sleeping over my house and my father walked into my room and kissed me goodnight. I didn't think much about it at the time because that was our norm. Dan, however, was touched. It was then that he told himself that, one day, when he has children of his own, he would kiss them and not be apprehensive to share his affection with them. Dan told me that he is that way with his two sons and one daughter and is very close to all of them. He said that my father influenced him as a child and that influence helped him become a good father today. Those are the lessons he is now teaching his children, who will, subsequently, teach their own. That is the memory that Dan has of my father. Once he told me that story, I realized that I am also very affectionate with my daughter and she with me.

The point is not that being affectionate is the only approach for children rearing; that is my preference, right or wrong. The point is, however, that as an adult and most certainly as a parent, mentor or teacher, we have an obligation to our children to inspire them to make good decisions. This is an important and proper child rearing approach. We must lift their spirits, lead by example, and promote his or her character when they inevitably get confronted with his or her crossroads. What experiences and lessons will they be pulling from when you are not around to direct them? Worse yet, could they possibly be better off without your ill guidance? Like each of us, they have the ability to be great and inspire others. Unfortunately, they also have the potential to create havoc in other people's lives. This is the reason it is so necessary for each of us to nurture our children and make good decisions within our own life, so they can be witness to our goodwill and integrity. They are watching us and we must communicate our actions accordingly. If you are not living a life full of meaning and helping your children learn the importance of love, kindness, compassion, and respect, then you are wrong. If you are not leading by example, you are doing a disservice to society, your family and your child. There is no more straightforward way to communicate the following about your shortcomings except to bluntly write: you are wrong!

What is the meaning of life? Living a life full of meaning. Build our children up one at a time, by first building yourself up to live a life full of meaning. Adults give children their foundation by what they are verbally and nonverbally communicating to them. If the foundation is weak, our children are more liable to plummet. They are more liable to plummet down the hole that we dug. If, however, the foundation is one of great strength, it is then that the possibilities become infinite. Be magnanimous and inspire others to follow your path. If, along this great journey, you know where to look, you will become witness to everlasting rewards. Along this noble path you will be the beneficiary of wondrous sights and, as a companion to each step that you take, will be mountains of joy and oceans of love. Climb your mountains and swim your oceans every single day of your life. There is no better way to answer the question, "What is the meaning of life?" then to "live a life full of meaning" by way of your actions. With Christ in your heart, reach, be great and inspire as you REACH Presentation Skills in an inspirational fashion.

What follows are my final remarks. I believe that it was important to write this closing section because it is about three individuals who have successfully communicated to others the importance of living a life full of meaning. It is important to take the time to read about these individuals because the paths, which they chose to walk, prove that my aforementioned words are so much more than simple words. These three individuals are proof that each one of us can make a difference in other people's lives by placing our personal signature across someone else's heart. The people that you elevate will then be in a better position to help another. It is the teamwork of life. Be like these three individuals and countless others and fight back the evilness that invades our world by lifting the spirits of others. Finally, allow others to sense your presence long after you're gone by communicating inspiration today! Become a smoldering wick upon a scented candle.

MY FINAL PARADE

I once lived a fairytale from beginning to end
And I found, on each page, my closest Friend.
He was guiding, teaching and sharing with me
His Love, wisdom and empathy.

I could always feel Him; we were never apart.
I could feel Him deep within each beat of my heart.
A glimmer of heaven was certainly inside me.
(Now that I'm gone, I pray He'll agree!)

I'm ready, my Friend and I'm not afraid
To commence with my…Final Parade.

Peter Carbone

You can sense a single flame's presence upon a scented candle long after that flame has been blown out. This is due to the smoldering of its wick. So many people have lived their lives in much the same manner; the ultimate example is Jesus Christ. What He accomplished during his life, humanity has sensed ever since. His physical presence has been "blown-out" over two thousand years ago, however, the influence of His life continues to be sensed by mankind.

> *"Therefore everyone who hears these words of mine and puts them into practice is like a wise man who built his house on the rock. The rain came down, the streams rose, and the winds blew and beat against that house; yet it did not fall, because it had its foundation on the rock. But everyone who hears these words of mine and does not put them into practice is like a foolish man who built his house on sand. The rain came down, the streams rose, and the winds blew and beat against that house, and it fell with a great crash."*
>
> MATTHEW 7:24-27

Within these final remarks, I would like to summarize three incredible and unique people who, not only persevered and succeeded for themselves, they persevered and succeeded and that success aggregately has helped thousands of lives. These people, for whom you are about to read, are people whose lives would have been deeply missed by thousands of people, if they never succeeded or if they failed to become the people they lived to be. If these three people failed to work towards reaching their potential and were unable to effectively communicate verbally and nonverbally, the consequences for scores of people would be unimaginable. These are three people who clearly were able to communicate with others in a magnificent manner because they lived magnanimously. They were inspirational by following their sublime inner universes. These are the kinds of people who have *smoldering wicks*. These are the kinds of people who inspire other people to say:

"Thank God for their existence!"

Smoldering Wick Number One

Most people have come to know the first person by, initially, their taste buds. I will give you the *ingredient* to his success. See if you can figure out to whom I am referring.

⇒ Sugar
⇒ Milk
⇒ Bean of the cocoa tree

If you have not figured out who this great man is yet, see below for more delicious clues. What follows are some wonderful, tantalizing sweets he created from the year 1907-1939:

⇒ Hershey's Kisses
⇒ Hershey's milk chocolate bar with almonds
⇒ Mr. Goodbar
⇒ Hershey's syrup
⇒ Krackel chocolate bar
⇒ Hershey's Miniatures

Milton S. Hershey was indeed a great man. He was a man who persevered and learned how to exchange failure for success. Indeed, Mr. Hershey was a successful entrepreneur. He not only learned how to make chocolate, he learned how to manufacture chocolate to meet worldwide demand. Undeniably, he was successful, however, it was what he accomplished *after* his entrepreneurial success that gives him Smoldering Wick status. In fact, Mr. Hershey's delightful story is far *sweeter* than his incredible story of how he took his company from a caramel failure to a chocolate empire. In truth, once I learned more about the extraordinary life of Milton S. Hershey, I have learned that the successful and sweet ingredient to his life was not, in fact, sugar, milk and cocoa beans after all; the ingredient to his life was the *responsibility* he had assumed in:

⇒ Love for people
⇒ Family
⇒ Himself

Milton S. Hershey (1857-1945) truly lived a life full of meaning. He lived such an extraordinary life that it even exceeded his expectations and dreams. Sure he was a pioneer, always trying to break new ground and exceed his most recent accomplishment; however, nothing could prepare him for the level of love and admiration thousands of people would bestow upon him, long after his death (October 13, 1945).

Consider the words that the Oz used in the film *The Wizard of OZ*, when he inspired the Tin Man: *"There is no better gauge in determining if we have a heart by not the people we love but by how many people love us!"* It is easy to believe that Mr. Hershey is loved for all that he has done for others. It is easy to believe that he has inspired so many people long after his presence on Earth. His existence was as unique and sweet as the chocolate he imagined. He lived beyond his self-worth and brought more than *Hugs* and *Kisses* into our world because his existence allowed, and continues to allow, others the ability to communicate success. He was, in a word, magnanimous.

Milton S. Hershey's story, although as real as the sun on a warm summer day, sounds much like a fairy-tale; henceforth, I have a child-like inclination to begin his story with four simple words:

ONCE UPON A TIME...

...long ago, lived a very unique man with such incredible foresight and ambition that he would leave this Earth a much better (and sweeter) place than when he found it. He had the kind of spirit a Cowardly Lion would be willing to exchange blows for; he had the kind of heart a Tin Man would shed tears for; and he had the kind of mind that would cause a Scarecrow to "face a whole box of matches" for. Indeed, Milton S. Hershey's Spirit, Heart and Mind continues to permeate a town and its people like a sweet breeze blowing through a cornfield.

His life, however, was not always sweet. He was not born with even a small fraction of what he had earned up to the time of his death. He was born with a name (which is now known globally), foresight and a lot of potential. So, how did he meet his destiny? He lived a life full of meaning.

On June 1st, 1876, a young, enthusiastic eighteen year-old Milton Hershey started his exceptional journey, with a one hundred and fifty dollar loan trusted to him by his Aunt Martha "Mattie." This loan was the funding for his first candy store in Philadelphia. This, his first venture, failed and that failure was the cause for him to seek another four hundred dollar loan from his family. He went to Denver and worked for a confectioner and learned to use milk to extend the shelf life of the candy. He then went to New York where he made his own confections, and sold his candy on the streets. Once again, he failed, as he failed in New Orleans. He returned to Lancaster, PA, and this time got financial support from a friend who believed in Hershey and his milk based candy.

Harry Lubkeker helped Hershey, not for a financial reason as much as for a human reason; he wanted to help Milton Hershey succeed. Without Hershey's good friend, Hershey may have never been able to realize success. This is important to remember as you learn the number of people Milton S. Hershey has been able to help. Milton Hershey was put in the position to help others, not only because he first helped himself, but also because someone else was in the position to inspire and help him succeed.

By 1894, he was able to muster enough financial support to start his Lancaster Caramel Company called, Crystal A Caramels Company. Just before a final seven hundred dollar note and a five-hundred dollar note came due from the Lancaster Bank, one of which was a note that had Aunt Mattie's house as collateral, he received a large order for his caramels; success would soon follow. For Mr. Hershey, this was certainly a sweet day. Once he built and established the Caramel Company, he sold it to a major competitor for one million dollars. By the turn of the century, 1900, six years after he established his caramel company, Milton S. Hershey was considered one of the most successful citizens of Lancaster, PA.

He took that money and invested in the construction of a chocolate factory in a small farming town in Pennsylvania, called Dairy Church. This factory became known as "the factory in the cornfield." This decision to build a factory in Dairy Church, PA, is a landmark decision that would change the lives of thousands upon thousands of people. At the time, however, Milton Hershey, nor anybody else for that matter, could even begin to conceive the goodness that would echo into the future.

He gave the landscape a makeover that is beyond the realm of extreme. He built and cultivated a town, which attracted a capable workforce. He developed trolley lines, parks, homes, schools, hospitals, banks, the Hershey Trust Company, department stores, The Hershey Hotel, streets and neighborhoods. He even donated land for the development of churches. The town was named Hershey.

He became famous for, not only his chocolates, but also his innovative ideas. Mr. Hershey's manufacturing plants and assembly lines were surprisingly high-tech and revolutionary. As you could envision, his riches began to mount and he began enjoying the "good life." That is until one day when he looked at himself in the mirror and saw a man covered with diamonds and a flamboyant suit. That was the day he remembered his humble beginnings and, according to the documentary, never wore jewelry again. This was also around the time he met the love of his life, "Kitty."
Her love most certainly influenced his life. They did marry, however, they could not have children of their own. This is where Milton Hershey's life reaches new heights. This is the reason his story is monumental and magnanimous.

Milton and Kitty Hershey founded a home for orphans. It is called The Hershey Industrial School, which was first an institution for orphan boys. The funding of a trust, which he had established decades ago, protects the future of the school even today. Without a son or daughter to bequeath his great fortune, Milton Hershey solidified the future of the school by investing all of his stock worth a staggering, $60 million. Today, that trust is as strong as ever and so is the appreciation of many a beneficiary. In regard to the students, everything is paid for, even their college. It has given and continues to give orphans the ability to succeed and inspire others. The Industrial School gives people the opportunity to reach their potential. Thousands of children lived, and continue to live, lives that they would ordinarily only be able to fantasize about, without the successes of Mr. Hershey.

Milton S. Hershey gives thousands of people the kind of life that allows each of them the ability to meet his and her potential. If each of them does assume the responsibility to work toward their potential, they will, one day, be in the position to help others. They will be in the position to contribute a beautiful verse to this great story as time ticks forward. In essence, they will be in the position to communicate verbally and nonverbally, inspiration for others. Now, hundreds to thousands of people have the potential to be magnanimous.

…And so the story began with "Once Upon A Time," however, it does not reach, "The End." Due to Mr. Hershey's inspirational existence, the story perpetuates, as does the smoldering of his wick…

Touch someone's life by communicating inspiration so that they will be able to grow, meet their potential, and then realize their own inspirational existence.

Smoldering Wick Number Two: Ms. Shirley

This next "*smoldering wick*" is a person who is not as famous as Mr. Hershey; nonetheless, this does not mean that her efforts are any less *sweet*. I first learned about Ms. Shirley at a national company meeting. We were at a dinner function with approximately one thousand others in attendance. I had never met or heard about Ms. Shirley until someone got up on stage and began telling us the story of this remarkable woman. Not only has she experienced recent professional success, she has lived a life of professional success. Next, I learned how her drive and determination has successfully touched the lives of many people in a magnanimous way.

She, along with two other wonderful people, co-founded the Ministry of Windsor Village United Methodist Church, Windsor AIDS ministry (WAM). Their mission is to "address the unique challenges associated with AIDS and the African American community. As the AIDS epidemic gained momentum, the need for culturally specific services increased. In response, WAM became the WAM foundation, Inc., a 501 (c) (3) non-profit organization dedicated to providing specialized services and programs to African Americans living with AIDS in the Greater Houston area." They do provide service to any ancestries who seek assistance and they are "warmly embraced" by WAM.

The ministry was founded in 1989 with very little money. According to Ms. Shirley, by the end of the 2003, Windsor AIDS ministry has been able to gain over 5 million dollars of support, which help them organize programs and services. For example, the funding is used for education, outreach, professional counseling, and food to assist individuals who have AIDS.

The truth is, one could not even begin to imagine the dread and loneliness AIDS patients or a cancer patient must live with every day. To the one who does know, you must feel an ache that is so heavy and cumbersome, that it paralyzes your ability to even gasp for a breath of air. To the one who does know, I imagine you feel like a person who is out in the middle of a dark, cold, rainstorm with no shelter or garments for protection or reprieve. Yet, you also know the profound appreciation you have for the kind spirits who work to help you, like the members of WAM. You must think of such people as a very thick, warm and fluffy blanket wrapped around your cold and tired body; relieving your pain, at least for a while. Ms. Shirley, and people like her, is the strength a wounded spirit leans on for support as he or she fights, painfully, to take their next step.

The smoldering of the wick continues because people like Ms. Shirley lives magnanimously. I bet people say, "Thank God for Ms. Shirley's existence!" This must be especially true when it rains.

Hopefully, works like Ms. Shirley's will never reach…

The End.

WORDS

These words are for the one I genuinely do admire.
They're words like love and trust, which fill my desire.
They're words of happiness, kindness, and certainly joy.
They're words of elegance and goodness that I had learned as boy.

So let it rain…let it rain…let it rain on me;
these words will still shine, I have learned divinity!

When I scrape my knee and I hit my head,
I know you will be there to tuck me in bed.
The words of healing, comfort and most certainly grace
Are the words that embrace me when I see your warm face.

They are words so special that only you could create.
They are words of such wonder; you make my pain dissipate.
Now I sit here and ponder which words describe you;
I re-read this poem and I find all the words do!

So let it rain…let it rain…let it rain on me;
these words will still shine, I have learned divinity!
Peter Carbone

Bill is a middle aged Christian man who is blessed with a beautiful family, a good job and an optimistic and cheerful outlook on life. Whenever I had previously approached him, I could anticipate a warm smile, upbeat energy and friendly interaction. Just by speaking with Bill, one could easily say that he was "on top of the world!" and rightfully so. However, as many in the past have experienced and many others will experience in the future, you may be on top of the world as the sun rises, but come sunset, you may find yourself sinking in that same world's quicksand. Unfortunately, that was the case for Bill.

One day, while Bill was focused on one of those routine, daily problems, you know the problem, the type of problem that we all have and consider to be so big and important that we focus all of our attention on it. It was one of those typical problems that tend to sidetrack each of us from our respective priorities. And then, one day, we are forced to stop examining the details of our trivial problem and are reintroduced to the forgotten subtleties of our life. The microscope is ripped away from our eyes as we unexpectedly get confronted head-on with a real life problem. Suddenly, we see the big picture of our world and the delicate lives of our loved ones who create our world. Suddenly, we wonder how we lost sight of the big picture in the first place.

On January 22, 2007, Bill was introduced to a ground shaking reality that would change his focus for life. Shortly after sunrise of that particular day, Bill had been working on a trivial problem and had been quite attentive with that problem as he had been every other day, which would lead him to this particular day. Bill was working diligently on the tasks that would resolve that problem, which would inevitably take him to the next trivial problem that was seeking his attention. This was the nature of Bill's daily activities that would lead him up to that dreadful day in January, when he answered a life altering phone call that put those trivial problems into their proper perspective come sunset.

The news that would nearly shatter his existence was that his twenty-two-year-old daughter, Kay, had been diagnosed with Hodgkin's Lymphoma. This is the kind of news that has the potential to cripple a parent. We don't like to see our children hurt, frightened or sick. The death of one's child is regarded as the embodiment of a loving parent's anguish. If you are a parent who has been informed that your child has Hodgkin's Lymphoma, you might as well have God, Himself, descend from Heaven, forcefully throw you down to the ground, look you straight in the eyes and say with all sincerity, "Your happiness is no more! What are you going to do about it?"

Bill's actions communicated to his beautiful daughter exactly what he was going to do. His actions communicated to her that she should fight, and fight hard because he was going to be in full body armor, swinging his sharp-edged sword, fully engaged, right by her side. Bill's actions were communicating to Kay that, with her in his heart, he was prepared to fight Nemesis, the Roman god of Vengeance, until his heart would beat no more. Bill's action communicated to his daughter that he wasn't giving up hope, that she wasn't alone in her fight, and that she could count on him every step of the way, no matter what the fight would bring. Together, they did fight. Together, they would fall. Together, they would lift each other off the ground, pick up their sword and continue with their fight.

War Zone

There are times I'd like to lay down my sword.
I still fight alone…once again I'm ignored.
Why must it be I who is always alone
To continue my fight in this perplexing War Zone?

I hope that one day, someone else will bend down
To pick up my sword if it does meet the ground.
If you do pick it up…I hope you will fight
So, I'll finally be freed both day and night!

And, yet I hear you, I do, even thought I'm alone
Fighting assiduously in this perplexing War Zone.
It's the fear that's becoming too, domineering,
And the fear that I'm fighting with no one else caring.

At times I'm so tired, it's my soul that may fail.
I wish I could unshackle it and let it set sail.
These are the times that I'm all on my own,
Fighting my battle, in this perplexing War Zone.

IT IS HE THAT YOU'RE HEARING (SO YOU MUST
BELIEVE).
IT IS HE THAT WILL BE THERE FOR YOUR AWAITED
REPRIEVE!
SO WHEN THE BATTLE GROWS TIRESOME, LAY DOWN
YOUR SWORD.
YOU'LL FIND YOU WERE NEVER ALONE, YOU'VE BEEN
HEARING THE
LORD!

Peter Carbone
Summer, 1996

What follows is a letter from Bill, weeks after his daughter's devastating diagnosis, which illustrates some of the trials and tribulations of their fight:

Yesterday was a difficult day, my daughter again had to have her infusion delayed due to her white blood cells being too low. We hope to be back on track this week without any future delays. Thanks Fran for your advise! I received advise from others that I will be following up on as well, Thanks.

Today I was not motivated AT ALL to swim, I've been frustrated with my inability to get the 'swimming' part of the Triathlon. Fatigue, swallowing water, cramping, difficulty breathing; I've been receiving coaching from Team in Training but I just wasn't getting it.

I laid in bed this morning thinking, my daughter wouldn't mind if I skipped a day swimming, I thought I could make it up some other time, I could do something else for her today, many excuses entered my mind. Then I thought of YOU and the sacrifice you made, you could have bought your own loved one something with the money you sent, paid a bill, bought something for your home, anything other than donating your hard earned money. With that thought motivating me, I got dressed, went to the gym and today was a breakthrough day, from my first lap I finally got the rhythm down, I was breathing on both sides and I swam farther than I ever did before, I felt like a fish!! I finally got it and now have the confidence that I'll finish the 500 yard swim, THANKS TO YOU!!!

Racing for a cure,

Bill

Bill communicated to his daughter that she should keep fighting; his actions were his means of communication. Bill took the type of action that would be beneficial to, not only Kay and himself, but also the many unknown sufferers who don't have the ability to fight for themselves. Bill didn't lay down his sword; he ran to Kay's rescue and fought back by raising money for the Leukemia & Lymphoma Society. The manner in which he chose to raise money was via, participation in a triathlon; which consisted of biking, swimming and running. Although Bill moderately exercised in the past, there was a remote chance, at best, that he could develop into a tri-athlete; his daughter was aware of this fact, as was Bill. Indeed, as I reflect on this point, that amplified the message that Bill communicated to his daughter. The fight for both Bill and Kay was indeed daunting, nonetheless, victorious.

By May of 2007, after five months of grueling mental and physical training, Bill was able to successfully cross the finish line. He said the following: "The instant I crossed the finish line, I felt as if I had won the Super Bowl!" Not only was he able to successfully transform himself from a middle-aged man to a tri-athlete, in five short months, he was also able to raise over $65,000 in donations, which will give hope and encouragement to blood cancer patients. As for the best news of all, within approximately the same timeframe, Kay's ailment was in complete remission; she has been blessed with the disappearance of her disease due to proper treatment, many prayers, and an ocean of love, which Bill is happy to swim across. Not only is she able to live a healthy and normal life, she has since been discovered by Hollywood. She is playing one of the main characters in a movie. To quote Bill, "We went from bitter despair, to sweet feelings of victory...she beat it!"

Daddy,

You will never come to know how much you are appreciated. This triathlon that you trained months for was just a cherry to top it all off but you didn't even have to do a thing to show me how much you care. It was simply said in the hugs and kisses I got even when I was in the worst of moods. I will never know how to show to you my thanks & there is a reason God made you & Mom my parents because w/out you guys I don't know what I would've done. You have been my ROCK through it all. I'm so lucky to have you because you always come to my rescue.

I love you,
Kay

As for the whereabouts of Bill and Kay, you can find them back on top of the world where they are closer to the prayers of the many people that they are now assisting and, as a result, inspiring to say, "Thank God for his and her existence!" The smoldering of their wick continues as they live magnanimously. Hopefully, works like Bill and Kay's will never reach…

The End!

Our life on Earth is like a large and robust log feeding a blazing fire. After awhile, inevitably, that strong and robust log will become dust. At first, the log contributes significantly by fueling a fierce inferno; but after awhile, the log turns into a solemnly burning fire, which inescapably will slowly burn the last of its fuel into ash and dust, leaving other logs responsible for keeping the inferno ablaze. What will people inherit from your life once you leave? What will be your legacy?

I say, communicate your verbal and nonverbal actions to others by being great and inspirational! Bring goodness into the world and motivate others to see all the beauty of God's blessings. Inspire people to first help themselves to see the goodness life has to offer. Inspire others to search for a first faint gleam of heaven that could be found inside each of us. Then tell them the importance of helping others to realize the same. Pass your spirit, heart and mind forward like a baton in a relay race. Instruct someone else to the importance of the race as you pass that baton forward and help him or her with his or her strides until they no longer are in need of your guidance. Set them free to stride at their own pace and trust them to continue to pass the baton forward with even greater strides. Trust them to understand the meaning of life and trust them to live their life full of meaning as so many others have done and so many others will continue to do.

Most important of all, teach and inspire your children. At the absolute very least, do no harm to their future. Do not rob them of their God given right to be great. Do not rob them of their ability to inspire others. Be held accountable to your every word in your home, just as you are held accountable to your every word in a business setting. Inspire your children to live a life full of meaning by first living it yourself. Teach them by example; teach them with your actions. Be magnanimous. Remember to live a life full of meaning by recognizing your responsibilities.

> ⇒ *First and foremost, you must be intimately acquainted with Love, family and yourself.*
> ⇒ *Second, it is you that must assume the responsibility of maturing all three.*

As I am writing these final words, my little girl is seven-years-old. She informed me of two facts. The first fact is that man (Adam) was created before woman (Eve) and the woman is created from the man. The part that God took from the man to create the woman was his, "funny bone!" The second fact she shared with me is that, like many of her children's storybooks, the last two words of *this* book must read, "The End." Who am I to dispute either of her two facts? Being the supportive father that I like to be, I listen to all of her suggestions and heed her wise counsel, especially the latter. So, here we go:

If you have learned any one lesson from this book, I hope you have learned from the stories of people like Mr. Milton S. Hershey, Ms. Shirley and Mr. Bill H. These are people whose ambitions touched so many other peoples' lives in such a positive fashion. So many people continue to benefit from their lives. These are people whose lives are like one flame's presence on a scented candle long after that flame has been blown out. Their presence, each of their life, created wicks to smolder for others to sense...eternally. You too can REACH Presentation Skills with the purpose of inspiration and, like them, you will find that your *spirit, heart* and *mind* will never reach...

The End!

I ask myself:

Why must I continue to REACH?

(And then I remember)

*If my desire were measured by the drops of
my sweat,
a vast ocean would be wrought by which
even Poseidon would not dare cross.*

So I continue to…REACH!

(So must you!)

Peter W. Carbone
March 2004

"Enter through the narrow gate. For wide is the gate and broad

is the road that leads to destruction, and many enter through it.

But small is the gate and narrow the road that leads to life, and

only a few find it."

MATTHEW 7:13-14

His Beauty

Do you see?

Do you hear?

Do you feel?

…His Beauty!

Come on, close your eyes
Take a deep breath and realize!

There is more to life than the mighty dollar,
Or the big red car and the fancy collar!

There is more to life than that silly mink
Or the diamond earrings and your next drink!

Do you see…
In the mirror the person you are?
You are more than a big house and a shinny sports car.

Do you hear…
Your soul as it whispers to you?
They are words of wisdom to help you get through!

Do you feel…
Your heart as you experience grace?
This universe of yours is such a unique space.
This universe you share; it is also God's place.

Try just try and
you will see!

You will hear

And you will feel…

His Beauty!

Peter Carbone 2002

This page I dedicate to you.
This page is dedicated to those of you who wish to live a life of virtue. This page is dedicated to those of you who wish to see God's Beauty. This page is dedicated to those of you who wish to be great and inspire! This page is dedicated to those of you who wish to live a *life full of meaning*.

Finally, this page is dedicated to those of you who find you must continue to…REACH!

Find your POWER as your tears roll down your face.

Find your POWER as you witness a feather slow-dance its way down towards Earth, in its most unique and subtle way.

Find your POWER because you can be like the wind, as it moves colossal trees from side to side with its invisible strength.

Find your POWER, for it is your POWER that gives you your ability to:

Be Great and Inspire!

REACH Presentation Skills © 2007, Peter W. Carbone

References

Covey, Stephen R. (1990), *THE 7 HABITS OF HIGHLY EFFECTIVE PEOPLE*. Simon & Schuster.

NIV Counselor's New Testament and Psalms (1983). The Zondervan Corporation Publishers.

Stone, Patton, Heen (1999). *Difficult Conversations*. Viking Penguin and Viking Books

C.S. Lewis (1943, 1945, 1952), *Mere Christianity*. Macmillan Publishing Company

Hershey Park references from Hershey Park, Hershey, P.A.

WAM foundation, Inc., a 501 (c) (3)

http://en.wikipedia.org/wiki/Visual_learning

Bruce Lee, *TAO OF JEET KUNE DO* (1975). OHara Publication Inc.

Zig Ziglar, *Secrets Of Closing The Sale* (2004). Fleming H. Revell, a division of Baker Publishing Group

Footnotes

[1] Covey, Stephen R. (1990), <u>THE 7 HABITS OF HIGHLY EFFECTIVE PEOPLE</u>. Simon & Schuster, Pg. 187.

[2] Bruce Lee, *TAO OF JEET KUNE DO* (1975). OHara Publication Inc

[3] Zig Ziglar, *Secrets Of Closing The Sale* (2004). Fleming H. Revell, a division of Baker Publishing Group

[4] Zig Ziglar, *Secrets Of Closing The Sale* (2004). Fleming H. Revell, a division of Baker Publishing Group

[5] http://en.wikipedia.org/wiki/Visual_learning

Printed in the United States
100420LV00004B/283-360/A

9 781434 330390